Understanding The Border Collie

The Essential Guide to Owning Border Collies and Collie Crosses as Pets

Carol Price

Published by
Broadcast Books
4 Cotham Vale
Bristol BS6 6HR
Catherine@broadcast books.demon.co.uk
0117 9732010 fax 9044830
Reprinted 1999 & 2000

isbn: 187409286-9

Printed by Cromwell Press, Trowbridge, Wilts

6 Belvedere Rd Bristol BS6 7JG

Cover Photograph by Janet Baxter

Cover Design by Sava Fratantonio

Facing Page: Portrait of Kim by Carol Price

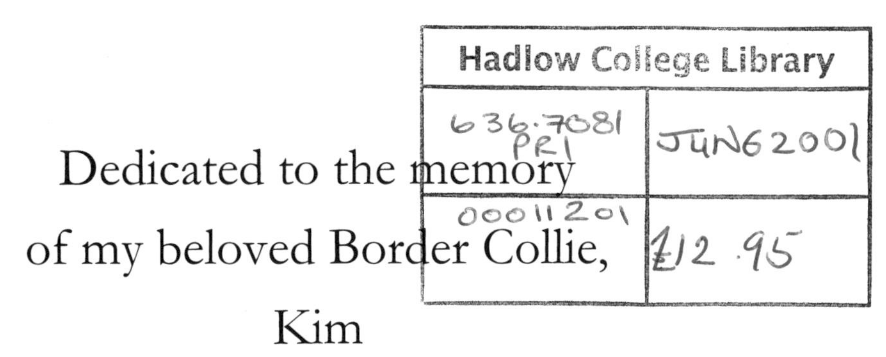

Dedicated to the memory

of my beloved Border Collie,

Kim

1982 - 1998

A TRULY EXCEPTIONAL DOG

CONTENTS

ACKNOWLEDGMENTS

In compiling this book, I would like to give particular thanks to the following: Tony Brenton and Colette Kase of the National Canine Defence League, for having such faith in the project from Day One, and for checking the text, Jennie Booth of The Border Collie Trust of Great Britain for similar support and inspiration, Jane Cresswell of The Border Collie Club of Great Britain, and John and Mary Gascoigne of the Southern Border Collie Club, and countless other individual Collie enthusiasts who offered their insights into the breed.

Finally, acknowledgments would not be complete without thanking my Collie, Kim, for so much original inspiration. Though she managed to stick a paw somewhere into each chapter that was written, sadly she did not live long enough to see the book actually published. But for a dog who experienced both suffering and redemption, and missed out on loving care and understanding for the greater part of her life, I like to think that she would see it as a fitting legacy.

INTRODUCTION

Treat me kindly, my beloved friend, for no heart in all the world is more Grateful for kindness than the loving heart of me

from : A Dog's Plea (Anon)

If you are reading this book, then the chances are that at some time in your life you have either acquired, or considered acquiring, a Border Collie or Collie cross as a pet. Like so many others in recent years, you have been attracted to the unique charms of this traditional British working breed; the intelligence, athleticism and apparent high trainability that mark out a dog with sheepdog genes.

Since 1976, when pedigree status was first allotted to Border Collies by the British Kennel Club, much else has happened to raise the Collie's popular profile. They are now a much-prized and increasingly sought after breed across the world due to their versatile talents and engaging looks. They have gained screen stardom in feature films like "Babe", and the televising of sheepdog trials has showcased their sharp wits and dazzling working prowess. It is also hard to think of any modern competitive canine event, like flyball, obedience or agility where Collies do not excel, if not dominate.

All in all, Collies can look like great dogs to have as pets. The only trouble is that in the rush to acquire them, too many people overlook the fundamental realities of their natures. They are dogs bred for centuries to be keen and tireless workers. This means they will not give you a quiet life. They have instincts that come ready-fixed and are not removable. Both mentally and physically they can react with incredible speed. If you want to keep a Collie as a successful pet, then you really must know more about what you will be taking on. And that is why this book has been written.

Collies are increasingly being seen as 'problem pets', because owners did not appreciate they could have drawbacks. The fact is that how good or bad they can be as pets will depend a lot on what you know about them. If Collies have become 'problem pets', then we have to ask why. We might have played a part in this with our unrealistic expectations, and by continuing to give disreputable Collie breeders a market for dogs that are less able to cope with domestic life, due to the way they were bred and raised in early life .

This book will explain the risks you can run through not getting your Collie from a good breeder. And why more 'problems' are likely to arise with Collies who come from less scrupulous breeders and more disadvantaged backgrounds.

When we look at all the Collies filling rescue centres in record numbers today - at one National Canine Defence League re-homing centre alone, Border Collies and Collie crosses account for 45.5 per cent of all residents - we know people are not understanding enough about these dogs. They do not understand their naturally excitable, energetic and work-driven natures, perhaps, or how to control and modify their instincts within a domestic setting while giving them adequate outlets elsewhere. They may not appreciate how such an inherently sensitive dog can become a deeply troubled one, psychologically, with inappropriate handling and over-harsh treatment. This book will deal with all these issues.

It is easy to feel compassion for misunderstood Collies, but sometimes one also has to feel sorry for the owners who could not cope with them. Few people start out with the intention of getting a Collie they cannot live with. All too often it happens because they have failed to estimate, or have never been advised of, the time, effort, energy, insight and commitment it would take to manage these dogs as successful pets.

Collies require a lot of thought. With more thought, and better advice, one can appreciate that a dog bred for centuries to work miles over rugged hills, to tirelessly herd livestock, to think and react as sharply as the wolf it is so closely related to genetically, will not slip effortlessly into the role of quiet and undemanding family pet, just because we suddenly decide that is what we now want. This book is for people who want to learn what it takes to be more successful owners of Border Collies or Collie crosses as pets. Who want to know why a Collie is what it is and does what it does, and how they can generally bring out the best in their dog.

We will focus on the Collie's history, psyche and inherent instincts. We will look at how to choose your dog, whether puppy or rescue inmate, and widely cover the world of Collie rescue. We must not forget the bleak and suffering existence so many Collies are forced to endure, nor overlook the ability of a Collie's crippled spirit to be healed in the right hands. We will also look at how to rear your Collie, feed it, train it and watch its welfare for maximum physical and mental health well into old age. We will look at how to manage and moderate the Collie's more energetic excesses and work with, rather than against, its intrinsic task-demanding drives. We will show you all the challenging competitive events you can involve your Collie in to give it outlets for its energies and talents.

In many ways this was the book I was looking for when I rescued my first Border Collie, Kim, several years ago. A book that would tell me all the possible downs, as well as ups, about this breed. I might then have realised why she was constantly to be found hanging off brooms, hoses or vacuum cleaners by her teeth, and 'eyeing' and 'herding' my cats with ceaseless intensity. I would have appreciated why even the removal of all four legs would not have stopped her wanting to chase any moving objects, small children included. I would have known the difference between a Collie showing 'dominant' aggression and a Collie showing pure stress and fear.

Kim was a Collie who suffered a double tragedy in her life. First to belong to original owners who mistook her natural Collie energy, spirit and sensitivity for 'stupidity' and all but crushed her soul, and second to be abandoned by them at thirteen years of age. The result was a very troubled dog. Much of what I originally learned about Collies, through her, was learned the hard way, and the rest through lengthy research and advice from many other owners, either with greater experience of the breed, or with problems that emerged as 'typical' in these dogs.

Since Kim, what I have learned most about Collies is that it just isn't enough to own them and tell them what to do. You have to earn their respect, win their confidence, give them a reason to want to put their faith in you. You have to know when to use patience and kindness with an anxious, stressed or fearful dog, and you also have to know when to be assertive, because there are few shrewder judges of wishy-washy leadership and unconvincing authority than this breed. Sadly, too many people think that being 'assertive' with Collies means resorting to physical abuse or punishment. There is no surer way to harm the psyches and confidence of these highly sensitive dogs, or to ruin any future relationship you might have with them.

There is no getting round the fact that making Collies into successful pets can be hard work. But as with all hard work put into a more testing cause, the rewards of getting it right can be enormous. In Kim I saw both how bad a Collie can be when starved of the most basic consideration and understanding, and how good it can be, and what it can achieve, in more enlightened hands.

There are so many Collies like Kim. So many can live their lives only ever realising a small percentage of their true potential, either because they have the wrong owners, or owners who never realised what their dogs could be. I would like to think that as a result of reading this book you will realise why so many people persevere so hard and so long with these dogs once smitten. The Border Collie really is no ordinary dog. It is outstandingly loyal, willing and courageous. It has incredibly versatile skills and an exceptional mind. It has grace and elegance, but also strength and stamina. There really is no other dog quite like it in the world.

Note: The term 'Collie' in this book, unless otherwise specified, is a broad term for Border Collies, working sheepdogs and Collie-crosses. Although they can differ according to breeding or registration (i.e. with The International Sheep Dog Society and/or the Kennel Club) many share similar genetic traits.

Chapter 1

WHAT IS A BORDER COLLIE?

Understanding Your Dog's Roots

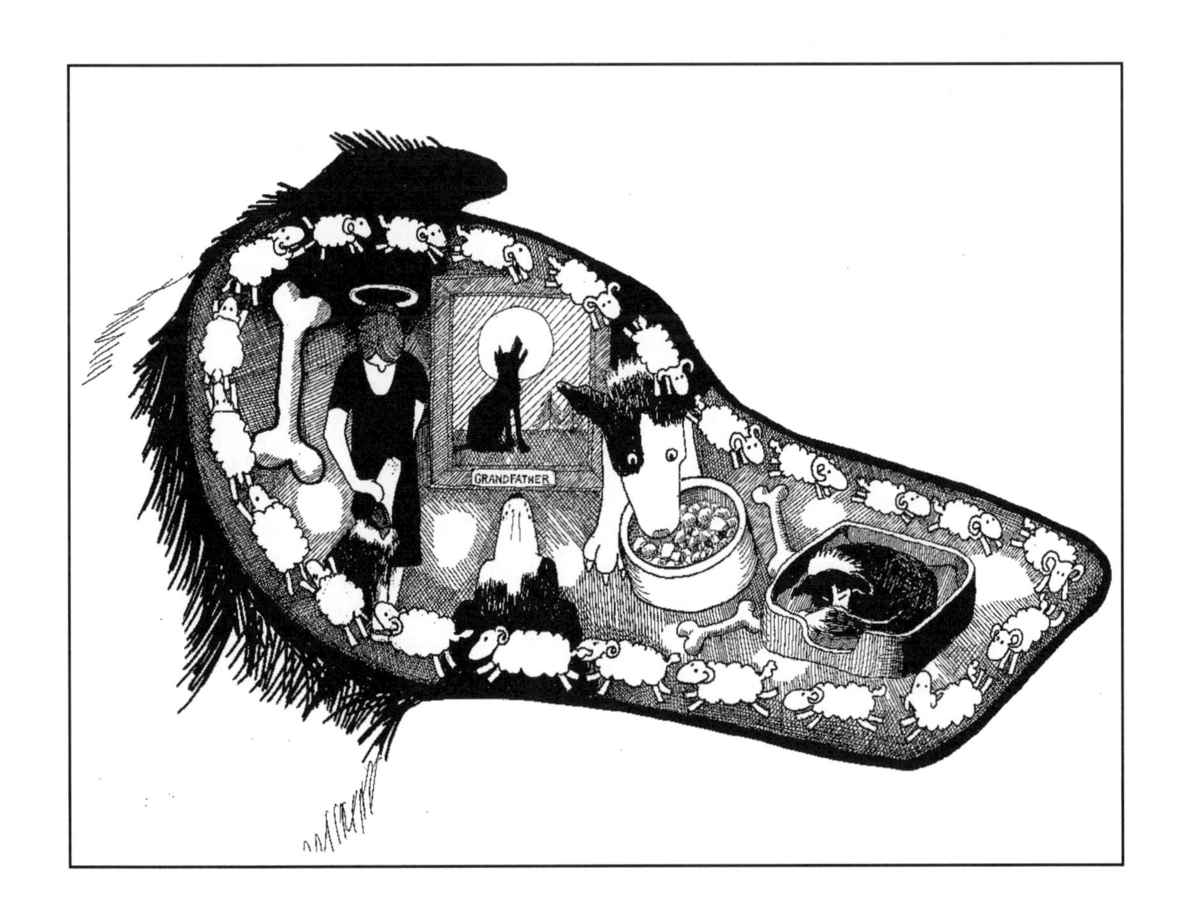

The more one understands about the Border Collie's origins, the easier it is to appreciate the difficulties it will experience adapting to a sedate and unstimulating domestic life.

Sometimes it is easy to forget how very quickly, in evolutionary terms, we have expected Collies to make the transition from working dogs to pets. Only three or four decades ago they were almost exclusively owned by farmers and herdsmen who kept them mentally and physically active all day.

Today's Border Collies have their origins in generations of dogs, over past centuries, who were selectively bred according to their skills at managing and herding livestock. Some of the earliest types of these herding and droving dogs are thought to date back to between the fifth and first centuries B.C., when they were worked by Celtic farmers in Britain and Ireland.

The 'Border' in the Border Collie's name derives from the grazing areas between England and Scotland where this breed was most commonly used. The word ' Collie' is thought to have been adapted from the Celtic word 'colley', which means 'useful'.

Watching a modern sheepdog about its natural work today, one has to marvel not just at its intelligence and grace, but also at the masterpiece of man-manipulated genetics it represents. A dog evolved to work with just one master, rather than within the normal canine 'pack structure'. A dog with all the stealth and herding instincts of the wolf, which plays a large part in its ancestry, but can still be commanded to contain stock rather than attack it. A dog with enormous stamina, agility and speed, who can think on its feet and turn virtually on a grass blade. A dog whose sheer force of character and mesmerising 'eye' can intimidate livestock many times its size.

There are farmers today who actively encourage new or would-be pet Collie owners to come and watch these dogs working in their natural role and environment. It not only gives a full insight into what Collies are capable of, given the right training and handling, but also makes it obvious that two brief strolls round the block each day are never likely to fulfil this breed's needs.

Before acquiring a Border Collie or Collie cross, you must be aware that many aspects of its behaviour are not 'bad' or 'aberrant', but simply instinctive within the breed. You cannot train natural and genetic instincts out of a dog, but you can, as we will cover later, find ways to modify them within a domestic setting, and give them some positive outlets. Meanwhile, here are just some instinctive behaviour traits that you might find in your Collie.

Eyeing

The term given when a Collie locks its stare on to an object, in order to make it move. The object in question could be your cat, a broom, or simply torch-beams and shadows. Basically anything that moves within the area of the dog's eye level can trigger the 'eye', and this includes small children. Whenever the dog 'eyes' the object and it moves, it is reinforcing a sense of reward; to the dog's mind, it has *made* that object move. Sometimes merely the anticipation of such a reward can keep Collies focused on objects for amazing lengths of time.

Chasing

What sheepdog would be worth its keep without a rapid response to fleeing livestock? If you put your dog in its normal working context, you would see how, in the farmer's eyes, the quicker a dog reacted in the pursuit of bolting or straying sheep, the more prized it would be.

Within a domestic setting such an instinct will still exist, even when it is seen by pet owners as inappropriate and quite exasperating. Especially when the objects it chooses to chase, in the absence of anything more appropriate, can include people, motor-bikes, other pets and cars. Again you must see things from the dog's point of view; as long as the object is still running away, he still hasn't finished his job. Often 'eyeing' and 'chasing' will run on in a constantly repetitive sequence.

Herding

Herding is naturally a vital part of a Collie's work. In order to move a flock of sheep or other livestock on to the right place, it must first be shepherded into a more manageable unit, with any stragglers pushed back into the main fold. Such an instinct actually stems from the wolf's natural method of hunting; pushing its prey into ever decreasing circles prior to attack.

However, when your Collie starts to turn its herding instincts on your party guests, it can be a surprise for the uninitiated. Likewise many pet Collie owners have found it hard to go out for a walk with other people and other dogs without their dog launching into a full 'rounding-up' procedure.

Gripping

This is the term used when a Collie, either to restrain a sheep or goad it on, will hold or nip the animal's back leg with its teeth. Such an instinctive function has led to Collies having a reputation as 'natural nippers'. It is not necessarily fair, as any instinct can vary highly in incidence from Collie to Collie. But it is something you should be aware of, together with the importance, from puppyhood, of discouraging Collies from any form of biting.

Dominance and Aggressive Behaviour

It is hard to imagine how a Collie with a basically weak and timid nature would crack it as a successful working dog. This is a breed designed to be able to goad and intimidate animals far bigger than itself into doing what it wants them to do, simply through its determination and force of character. As a result, many Collies can be quite dominant or 'pushy' personalities, and your training of them and how you organise your family 'pack structure' will have to take this into account.

Many pet Collie owners will also often find that their dog retains an instinct just to work for one master. In other words, their Collie will respond brilliantly to the one person it perceives as 'pack leader' in a household, but not so brilliantly for anyone else. For the sake of domestic harmony, and the dog's idea of where it should be in the family 'pecking order', this needs to be worked at and discouraged. (See Chapter 5: The Collie As a Family Dog). It should be up to you, not the dog, to set the rules of pack hierarchy.

Aggression in some Collies, though by no means all, can, if not suitably interpreted and handled, cause considerable strife for many pet owners. Due to the various and complex reasons for aggression in this breed, such as genetic inheritance, fear, stress or other factors, we will be covering this subject more fully in Chapter 6.)

Many owners of Collies as pets find it hard to understand why the working instincts in their dog remain so strong, when it hasn't been near a farm in its life - and neither had its parents, or even its grandparents. What they are overlooking is the ruthlessness of this dog's genetic history. Everything a Collie is today dates back to how its ancestors were selectively bred by farmers. What farmer would see the point in perpetuating the genes of a dog with little working instinct? So the genes of dogs with strong working instincts would have had a far higher chance of long-term survival. Today much is being made of the argument that it is better to choose a Collie with low working instincts as a pet. How well this theory would work for you depends on how skilfully you reckon you could select such a creature among a litter of pups or in a rescue centre kennel, in the absence of any expert advice. (See Chapter 3).

There are some excellent breeders today developing strains of Collie with temperaments more suited to domestic life, but not without controversy and criticism from some 'breed purists', who think a Collie should always be a working dog first and a pet or 'showdog' second. One can understand the protectiveness they feel towards this unique breed and its heritage, but we also have to consider the future welfare of these dogs realistically. If more and more Collies - as appears to be the case - are now destined for pet homes, rather than traditional working ones, how practical, or even kind, is it not to better equip them, psychologically, for this new sort of life and function? At the same time, as long as The International Sheep Dog Society is in business, registering and seeking to preserve all the best working Collie bloodlines, it is hard to imagine the genes of our top working dogs ever dying out.

We started this chapter by asking, what is a Border Collie? And in the main it is a dog still caught in the evolutionary throes of human demand. If it hasn't got enough working instinct, a farmer doesn't want it. If it has too much working instinct, it finds itself being rejected as a pet.

There are few dogs more eager to please than a Collie, but sometimes what we ask of them is just too much. Expecting to live happily with a Collie, without much understanding or leeway given to its instincts, will be about as fruitful as marrying a Martian.

In the human world, we expect to have to make concessions and adjustments and employ insight and effort to create successful relationships with each other. Somehow we tend to overlook how this is just as much a necessity in our relationships with dogs, who don't even share the benefit of a common language.

Hundreds of thousands of people across the world today have made a success of Border Collies as pets because they were prepared for the process of adaptation to go both ways. In the next chapter we will be looking at the qualities and circumstances required to make a good Collie owner.

Chapter 2

WHO SHOULDN'T HAVE A BORDER COLLIE?

Nobody likes to be told that they might not be the right owner for a dog or breed which appeals to them. However, Collies would not today be filling rescue centres and the clinics of canine behaviourists, and I would not be writing this book, if something was not so regularly going wrong between owners' expectations of this breed and the realities of living with it as a pet.

When we fall out with a dog, we often view failure only in terms of how that dog has let us down, overlooking what it was about us that failed the dog. And successful dog ownership starts with choosing a breed best suited to our individual circumstances and lifestyle. Generally, a Border Collie will not be the ideal dog for you if:

1. **You have never owned a dog before.**
2. **You have little time for exercise and training.**
3. **You have very small children (under the age of five).**
4. **You are elderly and not too active.**
5. **You are out of the house regularly for long periods of time.**

These rules are not always hard and fast. Someone who has never owned a dog before, but who enters Collie ownership armed with a great deal of commitment, knowledge and consistent resolve, can make a real success of it. However, generally following these rules might have spared much Collie/human trauma over the years.

Such basic guidelines apart, I think there are other realistic issues that have to be addressed in terms of an owner's individual personality. Border Collies are quick-thinking and fast-moving dogs whose natural working instincts (see previous chapter) can require rapid anticipation in order for them to be checked. For instance, anticipating when a Collie is going into 'chase' mode, and instantly giving a 'down' or other restraining command, can save you a two mile walk over the horizon to get that dog back. If you are not a person who can sustain a high level of mental anticipation, you had better be good at long walks.

It is frequently said that Border Collies are a breed requiring convincing leadership. Not everybody seems to know what this actually means and entails, or whether they have the qualities to fit the bill. Should they be doing a lot of stamping and shouting? Do you see many good shepherds doing this on farms?

Consider your own ideas of what makes a convincing and effective leader. Look back at your own formative years at school. The chances are you will have come across three basic styles of 'leadership' in teachers. These were:

> **The meek mannered and unauthoritative character** who you could play up no end, but who also made you feel insecure because they were meant to be in charge and didn't appear to know what they were doing.
>
> **The bully** who undermined your learning ability and confidence through constant criticism and shouting. The one who, by creating an atmosphere of fear and stress, made mistakes by pupils ten times more likely.
>
> **The inspirer** who naturally commanded respect through consistency of action and character, and who got the best out of everybody by giving them confidence in themselves and their own abilities.

The majority of the most brilliant and successful owners and handlers of Collies I have ever seen have, perhaps not surprisingly, qualities in common with the last category. They have the ability to make their dogs feel they are always doing the right thing for the right person, which is what most Collies want to feel. Often these owners and handlers were not born with such training talents. They had to learn them. They had to learn how to remain consistent when it was far less effort to be inconsistent. They had to learn how to get inside their dogs' minds.

You would not be reading this book if you had not already considered that a Collie could be the right dog for you. But are you really the right owner for a Collie? If you are still in the process of deciding, here are some helpful things to do:

1. **Ask friends who own Collies what the plusses and minuses are.**
2. **Ask any experienced dog owners you know how they think you would manage a Collie.**
3. **Ask rescue centres for some independent advice on the breed.**
4. **Read to the end of this book!**

Chapter 3

CHOOSING YOUR COLLIE

There are few things more appealing than cute Collie puppies, or homeless rescue dogs down on their luck. But decisions about choosing any dog have to be made with the head, not the heart. Too many dogs are chosen on rash impulse, or for sentimental reasons, with scant insight and forethought given to the long-term commitment and care they will require.

This is very tough on dogs. They cannot choose who owns them. They cannot know whether the stranger who suddenly takes them away one day will respect or betray their trust. We have choices they do not have. We can choose not to take on a dog we cannot care for properly with our circumstances and lifestyle, or choose to ensure that any dog we get will have the best possible home.

Collies are dogs which require high levels of effort, understanding and commitment The previous chapter will have given you some insight into what makes a good Collie owner, but here are more questions you will need to tackle before you even begin that trail to breeders or rescue centres for your new dog.

1. Why do I want a dog/this dog? Think hard. You should have some practical and convincing answers.

2. Does my partner/spouse/family feel as happy about getting a dog as I do? If not, depending on the strength of the opposition and in fairness to any future dog, you might have to think again. Collies monopolised by one owner in a household can cause problems for others in it. (also see Chapter 5).

3. Who is going to take the greatest responsibility for the dog's general welfare, feeding, walking, training etc.? How much time will this take out of each day, and can this time be spared? Again, caring and training of Collies is best shared by all the household.

4. How will this dog fit in with other existing pets, e.g. cats, other dogs, or animals your Collie might feel compelled to 'herd' and 'chase' without firm supervision from you.

5. Have you money set aside for any sudden major veterinary bills, or a good veterinary insurance policy?

6. Is your home really suitable for a boisterous young dog? What adjustments should you make to ensure your garden is escape-proof and prevent damage to more cherished and perishable domestic fittings and furnishings?

7.Who would look after your dog when you went on holiday, or in a sudden emergency?

8. Have you planned out everything your dog/puppy will need during its initial days with you, e.g. dog crate, bedding, food, toys?

9. Have you researched a good local vet, socialisatio or puppy training classes?

10. Finally, a last check on commitment. Your Collie could live up to fourteen years or more. Are you prepared to adapt your lifestyle to meet its needs and safeguard its welfare for that length of time?

Such a list will help you focus on what a new dog will require of you. If you were a dog, you would have wanted someone to have taken this much early effort to anticipate and accommodate your needs.

Puppy or Rescue Dog?

Puppies and rescue dogs have different demands, advantages and disadvantages. Both can be equally hard work. Both have the capacity to make excellent pets in the right hands and develop problems with a less experienced or informed owner.

The world of rescue Collies is a very busy one, covered at length later in this book, so for now we will be concentrating on choosing Collie puppies. Should you be thinking already, however, that a puppy will always be a 'safer' or 'better' bet than a rescue dog as a pet, don't forget that there isn't a rescue dog in the world who wasn't a puppy once.

Which Puppy?

There are many things you are going to have to consider when looking for a Collie puppy. Will you just want it as a companion pet, or are your ambitions also set on Agility, Obedience, Flyball, Working Trials or pedigree showing events? Different breeders (see advice section at the end of this book) will specialise in producing dogs for these varying disciplines.

If you wanted a pedigree dog, which could compete at the highest levels in the showring and Kennel Club licensed competition generally, it would have to be registered with the Kennel Club and possess the relevant pedigree papers.

You will often hear Collies referred to as 'working sheepdogs', which usually means they are crossbred Collies or Border Collies without any past registration history or pedigree papers. They can still, however, be put on the Kennel Club's working register (as 'Working Sheepdogs'), allowing them to compete in events like Obedience, Working Trials, Flyball etc. at Kennel Club run shows. Some Border Collies will be registered with the International Sheep Dog Society as well as the Kennel Club, illustrating a fine working heritage on top of pedigree looks.

Depending on what form of future competition you might be interested in with your Collie, the Kennel Club (see Advice section) can tell you which registration details are necessary. (Also see Chapter 10: The Competitive Collie.)

The Pedigree Puppy

The modern Collie can come in a varying range of sizes, colours and features, depending on its bloodline. Some dogs will, for instance, have pricked ears, whereas others will have ears tipping over at the top. Some Collies have one or two blue eyes, some will be larger or smaller than others. Coat colours, apart from traditional black and white, now include red and white, tricolour (black, tan and white), blue and white, blue merle, red merle and sable. Coat length also ranges from smooth to medium-long. Many dogs will also have the distinct 'mottling', 'spotting' or 'dappling' patterns through lighter areas of coat, which can be quite attractive.

One of the most engaging visual aspects of this breed, compared to others, is that no two dogs within it ever look exactly the same. However, a pedigree Border Collie will require a more distinct look, along with its relevant papers, to compete in the showring.

What sets the pedigree Border Collie apart from other Collie varieties is its conformation to a set 'breed standard' (or breed 'ideal') laid down by the Kennel Club. In theory today's pedigree show Collie can come in varying colours, but most top winners seem to be the much favoured black and white. The Border Collie breed standard will specify everything from the dog's height to shape of feet, set of tail and ears, movement, temperament and coat - white should never predominate.

If you imagine, however, that in a Border Collie pedigree puppy you could spot a future show champion, you would either have to be extremely lucky or an unrivalled expert. Even many top breeders can get it wrong at an early stage, as dogs continually change as they grow. And if a breeder was to suspect that he or she had a future champion within a litter, it is unlikely they would be selling it to you. Only about five to ten per cent of all pedigree dogs ever make it to the top of the show world, but you can still learn an awful lot, and have a fair bit of fun, in trying.

The 'Working Instinct' Factor

When looking for a Collie puppy as a pet, many people receive advice to choose one, as mentioned in chapter one, with a 'low working instinct'. In theory this sounds like good practical advice. You could imagine it to be a far less demanding dog within a non-working environment.

The extent of a Collie's working instinct can be a very hard thing to assess in the early days. Some young puppies will display some typical 'eyeing', 'herding' or 'chasing' instincts when only weeks old, but many others may not fully develop such working drives until up to a year old. So even experts can find many pups an unknown quantity, in terms of strength of working instinct, until they reach maturity.

Obviously, puppies displaying classic Collie eyeing/chasing behaviour when only weeks old have a high chance of becoming dogs with strong working drives. In the absence of such early evidence of working instinct, however, it may help to ask the breeder how he or she would assess the puppies. They might not want to commit themselves, understandably, to predicting how a puppy will turn out, but they have had far more time to study their litter than you.

They should also be able to tell you about the puppies' parents (dam and sire), and how strong or not their working instincts happen to be. But remember, just because a dog comes from a farm and working stock, rather than from a domestic home, it will not necessarily have high working instincts, anymore than the dog from a domestic home will necessarily have low working instincts. Genetic traits remain a very random and tricky thing to accurately predict in advance. So, while some breeders can claim to produce dogs with lower working instincts that might make better pets, it is nearly impossible for them to guarantee that they will all turn out this way.

This being said, however, one cannot overlook the fact that for many owners, the working instinct in a Collie is what makes it such a unique, challenging and rewarding dog. If you have a Collie without much working drive, and the sharp-wits and intelligence that often accompany it, what makes it more special than any other breed of dog? Also consider that a dog with low working drives can be at a disadvantage over others when it comes to the demands of competitive events, which push natural Collie working wits and talents to the full.

In short, if you think low working instinct is the most vital factor in any Collie puppy you are considering owning, you will find many breeders genuinely unable to point one out with any real certainty. They may also be rather baffled by your priority. Such a request is like asking for a dachshund that doesn't dig or a terrier that rarely barks. They might well suggest you should pick another breed.

Finding A Breeder

Anyone looking for a puppy will be advised to only get one from a 'reputable breeder'. This presupposes that they know how a less reputable breeder can be identified, which is not always the case. In the later advice section of this book, we will be telling you how to track down Collie breeders with a good name. For now, however, we will highlight some basic good and bad signs to look out for in a potential puppy source. First, the bad signs. These include:

1. Anywhere that produces large numbers of litters, particularly from many different breeds, each year.

2. Anywhere where you cannot see the pup with its mother and littermates. A pup on offer to be seen and sold in isolation from its family is invariably suspect.

3. Any breeding establishment where hygiene standards look poor or where the bitches look tetchy and ill-at-ease with their puppies.

4. Any place where puppies are raised in isolation from other people/animals etc. This deprives them of the vital early socialisation they need to develop later into well-adjusted adults. Do bear in mind however that when puppies are very young they are highly vulnerable to infection. Many breeders must therefore restrict and supervise any visitors from the outside, and perhaps also ask them to follow hygiene precautions to protect the pups.

5. Any breeder who does not ask you lots of questions about the life you will be offering your pup, the environment it will be living in, and how much experience you have of dogs, particularly Collies.

6. Any breeder who cannot convincingly answer any questions you might have, e.g. about the puppies' parentage, screening tests for genetic disorders (hip dysplasia, deafness, eye problems) or worming dates. Puppies need to be wormed at regular intervals from two or three weeks old.

By contrast, good breeders should offer the following:

1. Pups seen at home with their mothers, though for health reasons you will rarely be allowed to handle them under four weeks of age. Puppies destined to be pets are usually best raised in a busy, but not over-stressful, domestic setting. There is a fine balance between adequate early exposure to handling and the bustle of normal family life, and too much of it, triggering fearful responses in later life. Most experienced breeders know how to get it right.

2. Everything about the bitch's whelping environment is kept extremely clean. Both bitch and pups should look healthy and content. Bitches should never show fearful or aggressive responses to your approach.

3. A detailed fact pack on your pup. This should include pedigree details (where applicable), certificates (copies) of any past health screens on pups or their parents, worming details, a diet sheet advising how best to continue feeding your pup and any other helpful details or advice, from a good local vet to a puppy crate supplier, that will get you and your pup off to a successful start. A good breeder will be happy to supply all the after-sale advice and back-up you need.

4. The breeder should give the potential new owners a thorough grilling about the home they intend to give a puppy. Most good breeders have a nose for suitable owners of individual pups, and also for those they view as less suitable. If they do not want to provide you with a puppy, then respect that this may be due to reasons based on their own experience of where a puppy would thrive best. If the pup is a pedigree one, which the breeder believes has good showing potential, then they may want to keep it for themselves.

What Is A Good Pup?

As a rule, healthy and well-adjusted puppies come from places where much attention has been paid to early physical and mental welfare and development. Good breeders will also take much care over the dogs they choose to breed from, with an emphasis on sound temperament, constitutional robustness and past proven talent in showing, obedience or other special fields in which Collies excel.

Here are some good signs you should expect to see in your Collie puppy before you take it home:

1. Alertness and playfulness

2. Keen bright eyes

3. It should be dry, clean and wriggly, not damp or limp when you pick it up

4. There should be no evidence of eye or nasal discharges or diarrhoea

5. The tummy should feel firm and well-rounded, not light and bloated, which can be a sign of worms

6. The skin should also feel firm and elastic and not 'tent-up' when pinched (a sign of dehydration)

7. It should be feeding well and playing enthusiastically with littermates

8. It should be free from any visible deformities, (e.g. cleft palate) or para sites.

Much is made of which particular puppy in a litter you should pick; how, for example, the bold puppy that first approaches you tends to grow into a more dominant dog, and how the shyer puppy will grow into a rather timid and fearful adult, leaving the 'middle' dog as the best choice of easy-going pet.

Firstly, not everyone can have the 'middle' puppies. Secondly, such rapid early assessment is not always fail-safe. Thirdly, whatever puppy you chose, the part you play as owner will be hugely influential in the puppy's development. The 'wrong' puppy with the 'right' owner is likely to have a more successful future than the 'right' puppy with the 'wrong' owner.

Final Words of Caution

Although Collies in the main are a healthy and robust breed, they can be prone to some known genetic disorders, such as eye problems or deafness. At around 6-8 weeks, puppies need to be tested for deafness and Collie Eye Anomaly (CEA), which can later cause severe visual impairment or blindness. Other Collie disorders may only develop when the dog is much older. If this chapter has made you realise how much effort has to go into tracking down the right puppy, all one can say is just wait till you get that puppy home!

Lastly, it is very inadvisable to get two pups from the same litter. The chances are that they will bond more readily with each other than you. Puppies of the same sex can also start fighting as they get older, in a continual battle to be 'top dog'.

Most people have a set preference as to whether they want a dog or a bitch puppy. Both have advantages and disadvantages as they progress into adulthood, which we will highlight in Chapter 5.

Chapter 4

THE COLLIE PUPPY COMES HOME

Raising a well-behaved dog, like a well-behaved child, takes effort, patience and consistent application. Only the brave, or those blessed with exceptional stamina, would attempt both at the same time. This is why, as mentioned earlier, trying to raise very young children and energetic Collie puppies together in the same household is not generally advisable. Words like 'mayhem' and 'exhaustion' will rarely be far from your lips.

However, puppies and young children do have quite a few things in common. Both need the security of a routine, e.g. when they can eat, sleep or play, and guidance as to what is acceptable behaviour. (And please note that just as you would not leave a puppy in charge of a child, it is very important that children should not ever be left alone to look after a puppy, or be made responsible for the animal.)

When giving this guidance, the hardest thing of all is to be consistent in the rules we lay down. When something is alright to do one day, but not the next, we are giving rise to confusion and the notion that our authority can be open to challenge. This is a very bad notion to be implanting in any growing dog's mind.

One of the commonest mistakes we can make with puppies is allowing them too long a period of early undisciplined indulgence. We imagine that because they are so cute, small and endearing, they are too young in the first couple of months to be taught the difference between 'right' and 'wrong' actions. Unfortunately the reality is that when you let a young puppy continually do what it likes, e.g. 'mouth' or 'play bite' people's hands, chew your belongings or dig up the garden, it tends to grow into an adolescent dog who expects to do the same. Only by this time its teeth will be even bigger and sharper and its confidence to challenge you much greater.

Collies are dogs who will want to establish who is pack leader from day one. Make sure it is you. Make sure it will always be you and other members of your household who will set the agenda for what your Collie can and cannot do, and not the dog.

Early Days

One of the first useful things you can do when getting a puppy is to buy a book you can use as a daily record, or diary, of its progress. Each day you can enter a wide variety of information and details, from eating habits and toilet training progress to any possible health worries or experiences it has reacted to positively or negatively. You can also record its growth with lots of photos.

Apart from being fun to compile, this book will be a highly valuable tool in the dog's later life, should it develop any medical or behavioural problems. You and a vet and/or behaviourist will be able to look back at it as a vital guide to what might have gone wrong. Once it has grown up, it is all too easy to forget the formative experiences and events that might have shaped our adult dog's nature and personality. Sometimes events that seemed highly insignificant at the time, e.g. a passing scare over a noise or person, will have had a far greater impact on the growing dog.

The Puppy Crate

Another vital initial accessory will be a puppy crate or indoor kennel. This will need to be big enough to comfortably accommodate the dog in adulthood. For most Collies this means it should be an absolute minimum of 31 inches high. Dimensions available (length, width and height in inches) of 42" x 28" x 41" or 48" x 31" x 34" or similar proportions should provide a comfortable amount of space for an adult dog. Most vets or breeders or canine papers/magazines can give you details of good crate suppliers who will deliver them to your home. Ensure that they also come with a removable and easy-to-clean plastic tray on the bottom. Some crates can even be adapted to your car for travelling.

Many people have the idea that crates are an unkind form of confinement, which they certainly are if used wrongly. Puppies should always view them as a cosy, happy and secure little retreat, never a 'sin bin' they are thrown into the minute they appear tiresome. The crate should not be used as a prison for your dog to languish in for hours because you cannot, or don't want to, give it the level of interaction and attention it needs. A dog should never be left in a crate for longer than four hours during the daytime, as an absolute maximum; two to three hours would be more acceptable. At night it should not be left for longer than the extent of its bladder control.

The most important thing for the puppy is that it views its crate as a positive, comforting place and not a negative place of punishment and loneliness. Here's what you can do to encourage the positive view:

1. Leave the crate door open and initially encourage the puppy to go into it for small periods of time. Each time it does go in reward it with a food treat or something to chew and make a fuss.

2. Put some comfy, easy-to-clean bedding in the crate for the puppy and some small cuddly toys. Make sure there is nothing on the toys a puppy could chew off or swallow. The toys should not be small enough to swallow.

3. Many breeders suggest that you leave a cloth or item of clothing with your scent, or the scent of your house on it, with the puppy before it comes to your home, so that it will not seem so strange. You can leave this in the crate in the early days. Do be careful, however, to rule out the possibility that your item from home could bring in any kind of infection - discuss this with your breeder. Obviously the clothing you bring back with the puppy will also have the advantage of smelling of its former family and home, adding more comfort.

4. Always feed your puppy in its crate, and give it any treats there.

5. To aid toilet training, you can put a 'soiling area' in the crate for it to use. Newspaper is easiest to use for this purpose, but you don't want to get the idea into your puppy's head, when older or out of the crate, that whenever it sees newspaper it is permissible to foul on it. A litter tray filled with either earth or cat litter is a better option, because it is more like the natural outdoor surfaces a dog can expect to use for toilet purposes in adulthood.

6. Encourage the puppy to sleep in the crate. Puppies like to sleep a lot, especially after frantic bouts of activity or a good meal. Both will also usually trigger a need to go to the toilet. Once it has done this, preferably outside, and appears dopey, tuck it up in its crate bed. Until the puppy seems totally happy and at ease in its bed, leave the crate door open, except at night when you do not want it to wander.

Crates can also help limit the chewing of your possessions, household furnishings, and highly dangerous items like electrical cables, poisonous house plants or other objects your puppy could swallow to harmful effect. Remember that puppies, like children, have a lengthy, curious period of wanting to stick anything they see into their mouths! This peaks when they are teething at around four to six months.

It is very important for the puppy to realise, early on, that it cannot just chew anything it wants to, when it wants to. When, out of its crate, it begins to chew anything around the house, immediately put it back in its crate. Do this gently, with no shouting or punishment, and give it its own 'personal' chew item to work on instead. This should be a special chew toy or hide chew. Praise the puppy fulsomely when it chews the 'right thing'.

If this is done repeatedly and consistently, the puppy should eventually get the idea that it can only chew its own item in its own kennel. Anything else represents your item in your kennel and is out of bounds.

However, in the early days, try to restrict how much time the puppy has to spend in its crate. It needs plenty of time to play, interact with people and other animals, and generally discover and explore the big wide world outside. This is how a puppy makes a successful transition into adulthood. It does not do it sitting for hours in a crate. Initially, these should be the main times when your puppy will need to be in its crate:

1. **When it is in need of rest**/sleeping, including at night.

2. **When it needs to be kept out of danger,** e.g. when you are engaged in any task where the pup could be tripped over or have access to dangerous chemicals. Also any occasion where the front door and/or gate into the road is continually kept open, e.g. workmen/delivery men visiting. It is all too easy during such a commotion for a puppy to run out unnoticed into traffic outside. It should also go without saying that a back garden any puppy has access to should be escape-proof.

3. **When it is being fed**/having treats/chewing.

In this way a puppy will realise that the crate is a place where only nice things happen, and where it can feel safe, secure and untroubled. If you get this positive association right, then eventually it will be happy to spend more and more time there of its own choice.

Playing and Learning

Setting regular intervals aside to play with your puppy is a vital early consideration. Remember, prior to coming to its new home, much of its previous social interaction was with its litter mates, interspersed with the odd bout of maternal discipline. While good breeders do their best to acquaint puppies with being regularly handled by people from an early stage, you will need to take this process much further to establish strong bonds between the growing puppy and all other members of the household. This is best done through the enjoyable medium of shared play.

Play sessions have to be managed correctly, or you could end up with the puppy learning quite the opposite lessons from the process than those you intended. Puppies that were too roughly handled or hurled around in their early days, or that were allowed to nip excessively, or allowed to win all the games and be possessive over toys during play sessions, all too often grow up into more problematic adult dogs.

From the minute you begin playing with your Collie puppy, you need to have two objectives in mind. First, you want the puppy to get the idea that you are always an enjoyable person to be with, ready to provide it with treats, playthings and happy experiences. Second, that you are in charge of what happens during play, and that you own and control all the best toys.

Puppy toys do not need to be complicated or expensive. Many owners can spend a lot of money on popular play cubes and cotton 'tugs', only to see their puppy derive ten times more pleasure from an empty yoghurt pot, plastic flowerpot, and the cut-off leg of an old pair of jeans. Be careful about thin plastic pots, however; the minute they crack, take them away to avoid the puppy swallowing any sharp fragments.

Some say that a puppy should never be allowed to 'win' any games with you from the start, be this over possession of a 'tugging' item, or any other. But how long would you want to play a game that you could never win - and how much fun would that be? Being allowed to win sometimes will keep a puppy's interest in the game - and in playing with you - alive. The most important thing, however, is that the puppy learns to 'leave' or let go of a toy when you ask it to, especially when it has become particularly heated or over-excited.

Depending on when you start working on this exercise, it may take time for the puppy to understand the term 'leave', and to let go of an item. Persist, but always stay calm, yet firm. Too much frantic pulling and shouting will work the puppy up even more, or provoke some form of retaliatory or defensive aggression, as it becomes frightened by your sudden hostility. With enough patience and firm persistence the puppy should eventually let go - at which point, praise it fulsomely and/or give it a treat. Routinely repeat this exercise until the puppy lets go of an item on command.

Just as you should always be the one to initiate play sessions, you should also be the one to end them. When excessively stimulated or excited, puppies do not always know when to stop exertion for their own good, so you must curtail sessions before they get over-tired. Young puppies, just like young children, can be at their most 'manic' when near exhaustion, and you will soon learn when to intervene to stop a play session reaching this stage, and allow the puppy to wind down and rest.

Within your household, you should establish the same 'rules of play' for everyone entering into games with the puppy, so that it always knows the boundaries of what it can and cannot do with all family members. This way there will also be a consistency of approach among all those 'higher' members of the puppy's 'pack'. Children, especially, need to learn to play with puppies gently so that they will not frighten, threaten or over-stimulate them. Surprisingly, many children can understand and respond to such an approach to something even smaller than them.

Nipping

In the context of play, and during everyday handling, Collie puppies can often be excessively over-active with their teeth. It is a natural part of normal puppy 'play' behaviour, but not to be encouraged. As their teeth grow bigger and sharper, they can deal out some painful nips. When this happens, you will have an overwhelming desire to retaliate, but resist at all costs.

It may well be that within the dog's natural pack, a puppy will be physically reprimanded for such behaviour towards its mother or other 'superior members', but few humans, I feel, could replicate the swiftness and subtlety of such dog-to-dog discipline in a way that wouldn't frighten the puppy, undermine its trust in you, or cause it to become more defensively aggressive.

When puppy nipping occurs, the best thing you can do is to yell 'ouch!' or 'No!' loud, then walk away from the puppy instantly. The same applies when it nips during a game; abandon the game immediately and walk away. Eventually the puppy will understand not only that its behaviour is unacceptable, but that nipping brings about a cessation of all social interaction and fun activity. For most puppies, this is a pretty big and usually very effective disincentive.

Establishing good 'dog-to-human' bonds apart, some of the most vital early commands and exercises, such as 'sit', 'wait',' 'leave' and retrieve, can be learnt by Collie puppies in the context of play. Always encourage a puppy to share retrieved toys with you, and praise it well for doing so by letting it play with the toy for some time before taking it away again. Such encouragement and reward will pay dividends later on as you progress on to more formal and complex retrieval exercises.

If your puppy is always happy to play with you, share its toys with you, let go of them when you ask and bring you back anything that you throw, with instant and enthusiastic willingness, then congratulations! Your play is progressing pretty well.

Socialisation

Many less experienced dog owners treat the notion of 'puppy socialisation' with a level of confusion and misunderstanding. They think it is just about puppies meeting other puppies in special classes. They do not fully understand why it is so vital a concern in a dog's early life.

Conclusive research into canine behaviour now makes it clear that the optimum time for a dog to confront, and successfully adapt to, new sights, sounds, experiences or events is within its first fourteen weeks. Within this time, providing its exposure to all unsettling new stimuli is properly handled, and the puppy is never encouraged to be afraid, there is a high chance it will accept them as a normal and unfazing part of life. After these initial fourteen weeks, the likelihood of this happening progressively diminshes. There is a much higher chance of a dog's fearful reaction to new sights, sounds or experiences staying with it for life.

With Collies, due to their high level of sensitivity as a breed, early socialisation to a variety of new experiences can seldom start soon enough. It is sadly no exaggeration to state that early bad handling and lack of socialisation of Collies is a number one reason why they later turn into 'unmanageable' or unwanted dogs.

Some Collie puppies will always be more naturally easy-going than others. Some will react more strongly than others to any given (and potentially threatening) new sight, sound or experience. As the owner of a new Collie puppy, the uppermost thought in your mind will be to expose it to as many novel experiences as possible without the 'fear response' button ever jamming fully down, storing up problems for its later life.

Start this project as soon as possible. Obviously your puppy's full integration into the outside world, on a lead, cannot begin before it has completed its vaccination programme, which usually starts from around eight weeks onwards; your vet can advise you when your pup is likely to have full protection. But you can start carrying it around when it is very small, introducing it to sights and sounds like traffic, trains, other people, children and assorted animals. Things that we find very commonplace, like people in hats, horses, sirens, lorries or building sites can be immensely unnerving to an inexperienced puppy.

When your puppy is exposed to all these experiences the most important thing is not to let a fear response get rooted. It is a natural reaction to want to soothe and make a fuss of a puppy when it looks frightened, but unfortunately the message this usually gives to the pup is that it is right to be afraid and we are rewarding it for that reaction.

It is far better to ignore any frightened-looking behaviour and instead to 'jolly' the puppy along. Make light of its reaction and distract it with a toy or game or titbit. Give it something nice or fun to do, make it clear you are totally unbothered by whatever appears to be frightening the puppy. Eventually, especially when backed up with a nice game or food treat, it will be inclined to follow your cue.

The importance of properly socialising your puppy with other dogs is sadly often only apparent in its later life. A dog who lacks a properly learned 'etiquette' to succeed in normal canine social interaction is not only denied the fun of knowing how to engage in play with other dogs, and thoroughly enjoy their company, but it is also far more likely to get attacked or involved in fights. This is because it will not necessarily know how to properly 'respect', in terms of body language, any dog it meets of 'higher-ranking' status. The higher-ranking dog may well see this as a challenge.

Most adult dogs are quite tolerant of puppies, while at the same time making it clear when a puppy's behaviour has become too disrespectful or annoying. Puppies can learn an awful lot about acceptable behaviour from adult dogs. Let them learn it. Do not be constantly intervening when an adult dog gives your pup some form of reprimand, unless the dog , as can be the case in rare circumstances, looks dangerously aggressive. The older pups get, the less tolerant adult dogs will get towards their 'silly' and 'pushy' behaviour. Eventually the growing puppy will realise that if it wants to play in another doggy 'gang' it will have to fit in with that gang's hierarchy and rules, or it will be shunned and ignored.

Puppy socialisation classes, where puppies can exclusively play and socially interact, are also useful. Many owners move on from these to more formal dog training classes. Your vet should help you locate both types of classes in your area. (If no joy, see the Advice section at the end of this book.) In short, good early socialisation means you are giving a dog its best chance to be well-adjusted and socially confident in later life. When a dog has developed the confidence not to feel threatened by any new person, child, dog or experience, it will also not have a compulsive desire to respond to that threat - which in many cases can mean with aggression.

Collies as a breed will commonly - with the exception of when they are responding to a hunting or 'gripping' instinct - use aggression in a defensive, rather than offensive, way. This means their aggression is frequently triggered by something or someone which has badly frightened or threatened them in the past. The next time they catch a whiff of any situation/person which reminds them of this fright/threat, they are likely to try to get a self-protective attack in first. Much more about aggression in Collies will follow later in this book.

Meanwhile, the two other chief experiences that will need to be a part of your puppy's early socialisation will be a trip to the vet and car travel. A trip to the vet with a new puppy is always a good idea for an overall health check, and to discuss vaccination and worming programmes. (As a rule, puppies begin their vaccination programme at around eight weeks. They are usually wormed first at around three weeks old and will then have to be wormed again at fortnightly, then monthly, intervals, up to the age of six months. Thereafter they should be wormed every six months.)

Bedtime

Most puppy owners will tell you that their new charge's first few nights with them are always the most traumatic. Imagine how the puppy must feel. It has suddenly left a wonderfully safe and secure environment, the protection of its mother and the company of its litter mates to be on its own with strangers in an unfamiliar place. It will naturally feel insecure, wary and frightened.

Opinions can differ on where puppies should spend their first night. Some now believe that the traditional method of leaving a puppy downstairs, and ignoring its whimpering protests about sudden isolation, is too harsh, and that instead, a puppy should spend an initial night or two in a box or kennel in your bedroom, before being gradually moved away - if desired - to a more distant spot later.

However, the snag with Collie puppies who start sleeping in the bedroom on night one or two is that they tend to want to go on sleeping in the bedroom, and don't always take kindly to being moved elsewhere later on, with just as much - if not more - whimpering protest at the prospect. So what has been achieved?

No transition from pack to isolation is ever going to be easy for a puppy. But the difference between a puppy who has slept downstairs on its own from day one, and one that is moved from the bedroom to somewhere else, is that the one downstairs has no memory or expectation of being somewhere better, which a lot of extra protest might just get it returned to.

Providing a Collie puppy is left downstairs from the start, in circumstances that are as cosy as possible - with a hot water bottle, comforting cuddly toy, fleece bed and perhaps even a blanket - my own experience is that they settle down pretty soon after initial bouts of whimpering, which are entirely understandable. And rather than being 'heartless' at ignoring these whimperings, you are beginning the process as early as possible, and before other confusing precedents have been set, of the dog learning to cope with periods of being on its own.

Obviously, the ultimate choice of what to do on the first few nights is up to individual owners. But do be aware that Collies are 'rank manipulators' in the face of any privilege they like the look of and want to retain, and of any 'grey areas' of human resolve that they can push, with enough protest or guile, to their own advantage. Often Collies with greatest dominance and/or separation anxiety problems are those long used to the privilege of sleeping with owners in their bedrooms.

The exceptions I would make to bringing Collies upstairs at night is if they are sick and needing supervision, or elderly. Trusted and well-behaved old companions deserve a little more indulgence, reassurance and comfort. Otherwise, I remain convinced that downstairs is still the best and only place to leave Collies overnight.

Rules of the House

Where puppies sleep will be one of the basic 'house rules' you will need to lay down when it arrives. From the outset it will have to understand its place in the family 'pack', which is lower than any other family members, and what sort of behaviour will and will not be acceptable. These rules will have to be consistently applied by everyone. Here are some important ones to establish, recapping on some things we have already covered:

The puppy always sleeps in its own bed in its own place.

The puppy only has access to certain rooms.

The puppy always eats after other family members.

The puppy is never possessive over toys or other belongings and that you always initiate and end all games.

The puppy only ever chews its own items in its own bed/crate.

The puppy should not mouth or bite other people; discourage it whenever this happens by taking your hand away and yelling 'ouch!' or 'no!' and ignoring it for a while to signal your displeasure. When you yell 'no!' the puppy should stop what it is doing.

Encouragement

Do remember, however, that a puppy's early life shouldn't just be full of negatives. Make sure you praise it heavily, and instantly, the minute it does something right. Praise for something done right, like a 'no!' for something done wrong, has to be applied within split seconds of the action, otherwise the puppy is unable to make any association between what it has done and whether it was right or wrong.

Never use physical punishment on a puppy, however exasperating its behaviour. Contrary to a weird popular belief among some dog owners, puppies do not do irritating things 'on purpose', to 'play up' or 'try one's nerves'. They do it because they are puppies and know no better.

The easiest way to shatter a puppy's confidence in itself and you, and to turn it into an insecure, 'unmanageable' adult dog, is to blight its early weeks and months with constant physical and verbal punishment. Collies raised in this way frequently turn into stressed and 'mentally-fuddled' adults, lacking the vital confidence they need to think, respond and perform at their best.

In raising your Collie puppy, you should be placing greater and greater emphasis on everything it does right. If it sits when you want it to sit, comes when you want it to come, or leaves something when you ask it to, then really make a fuss and make it clear how pleased you are. When it does something wrong, pay little attention, unless of course the action, like biting, needs very swift early aversion therapy in the form of 'no!' But 'no!' should only be used for the most dire or dangerous misdemeanours, or its impact will soon be devalued.

Dogs are naturally socially co-operative animals. Most puppies want to please. Eventually, through the above tactics, puppies should learn that the 'right' actions are highly rewarding and the 'wrong' ones far less so. It therefore makes sense to do more 'right' things than 'wrong' ones. The dog has not been bullied into this choice. It has, even if unwittingly, made it for itself. This way its confidence in itself and you stays intact. There is no better Collie owner in the world than the one who has learned how to make his or her dog feel it is always doing the right thing.

Diet

When puppies first come to a new home it is common for them to have initial bouts of diarrhoea due to the upheaval. Sometimes this is also because they have been given a sudden change of diet, and for this reason, until the puppy properly adjusts, it is better to keep feeding it what it had at its last home, or what the breeder recommends.

If, despite this, the diarrhoea persists, keep the puppy on nothing but cooled boiled water for twenty-four hours, then give it something bland like chicken and rice or scrambled egg before gradually re-introducing its normal diet. This should do the trick, but consult your vet if the diarrhoea still persists.

Your puppy will need about four meals a day up to the age of three or four months. Thereafter it will need three meals a day until it is five or six months, and beyond that two meals a day. Many adult dogs are fed just once a day. It is a matter of personal preference and what seems to best suit the dog. My own preference, particularly as dogs get older, is for two meals a day, which places less pressure on the digestive system. Dogs, quite normally, will get into the habit of turning down a meal here and there to rest their stomachs. Unless they stop eating for a prolonged period, or have other symptoms like vomiting or diarrhoea, it is no cause for alarm.

Be aware also that dogs are naturally competitive feeders. In the wild they will descend as a pack on a 'kill', all vying to get their share. For this reason, and because your puppy will be used to competing with its litter mates for food, it may not eat well during its early days alone with you. This situation normally rights itself quite soon, but again, consult your vet if your puppy stops eating for a prolonged period.

There is currently a mind-blowing array of special foods on the market for growing puppies. Your breeder may have recommended one kind, you might feel you prefer another. Phase in any change gradually. In finding the best food to suit your puppy, and what it appears to thrive best on, trial and error remains the key. However, do not mix up different prepared diets, as this could result in your puppy getting either too much or too little of certain essential vitamins and nutrients. This means his or her intake will not be properly balanced.

Grooming

Regular grooming of a young puppy is vital for two main reasons. First, because it allows you to check out its skin and coat for any lumps, bumps, swellings, injuries or parasites and second because it gets the puppy used to being handled. Every day look in its ears, which may need a wipe with a special ear cleanser and a soft cloth, being careful not to poke anything anywhere down the ear canal. Also look in its mouth and throat, pick up its feet and look at its claws, check the eyes for any discharge or excess tears, and run a brush or comb over its entire body.

If you start doing this when a puppy is young it should present far less resistance to handling in adulthood. It is also quite a good idea start brushing your puppy's teeth two or three times a week with a very soft toothbrush and some bicarbonate of soda well diluted in warm water. Dogs who have not had their teeth attended to in puppyhood often find it an unnerving business in adulthood, and one they may greatly resist. But as about 80% of adult cats and dogs now suffer from some form of gum disease, the value of early attention to oral hygiene in pets cannot be underestimated.

Getting Used to a Collar and Lead

Make sure your puppy gets used to wearing a soft, comfortable collar early on, and then a lead. But do not instantly start yanking it round the house or garden on this lead, or allow anyone else to. The puppy needs to get used to the feel of the lead and collar gradually, not view it as a sudden and frightening torment. Harnesses are often better as they put less strain on the puppy's neck.

Allow the puppy to run round with the lead trailing loose for a while. Then, applying light contact, encourage the puppy forward on the lead, perhaps with a toy or treat in your hand. Get the puppy's attention and try to make it walk alongside you, rather than drag it along or let it pull in front. Practice this for short periods of time, rewarding your puppy when it does well. And be patient. You would not find it a very pleasant experience being dragged round the garden by your neck and shouted at. Neither does the puppy. Obviously you will have to get your puppy some form of proper identification at some time, either an identity disc, ear tattoo or microchip.

Getting Used to Car Journeys

As mentioned earlier, it is also an idea to get your puppy used to car travel early on. Start with small journeys of about five minutes, building up to longer periods. Initially these journeys should start and end at home. If a puppy gets the idea that a car journey means he is always going to go somewhere new and exciting, he will be more prone to get over-excited and car sick. By the same token, you do not want him to think a car journey means going to the vet. So keep making varied journeys. Sometimes you go somewhere new and exciting, sometimes you just go round the block and then home again, and sometimes you do, indeed, go to the vet. Keep the puppy guessing - then it won't know when to get excited. With Collie puppies, it is also *vital* to prevent them jumping against the inside of your car windows to bark at passing traffic, as this can rapidly become an annoying and highly distracting habit. The *instant* they attempt to do this, stop the car and tell them to get down. Do this *every single time* they try to jump at the car windows. If they still persist, you may have to make them travel tied down in the footwell of the car,or in a special car crate with a cover so they can't see passing traffic, until they stop the habit.

Puppies and Children

Although puppies are incredibly active creatures, they also need proper rest, free of stress, to develop healthily. Do not let children, or anyone else, over stimulate them during their early weeks and months, or permit games which might encourage the puppy to bite. Children must be taught that puppies are not toys. The puppy's need for peace and quiet when eating or sleeping must be respected. Children should be encouraged to take part in all the chores associated with raising a puppy, although they cannot be expected to take full responsibility yet. Puppies are a family project, as we will highlight in the next chapter.

Chapter 5

THE GROWING COLLIE:

Early Training as a Family Dog

In the first few months of life, your Collie will be growing fast and its mind will be like a sponge; it will soak up a vast range of new sights and experiences. It may begin to show some, or all of the Collie working instincts, such as 'eyeing', 'herding' and 'chasing' which can come as quite a shock within a domestic environment for those with less experience of the breed.

While it is unfair to get a dog with all the mental and physical energy of a Collie and never give it a chance to channel these energies in a positive way (of which more later), there are bound to be times when a pet Collie's boisterous instincts are going to be inappropriate and need to be controlled. You cannot have a dog who constantly feels at liberty to chase small children round the garden, savage any moving piece of electrical equipment, and charge out after any passing bike or car. Not only is it extremely dangerous, but it also gives the message that the dog is in control of its actions, not you.

Control of Collies by owners can never start soon enough. As the dog moves beyond puppyhood it will continuously test the boundaries of what it can and cannot do. Just like human teenagers, once the sex hormones start to surge, some Collies can become quite wilful and difficult adolescents. They will be even more difficult if they have got to this stage of their lives without their behaviour ever being properly controlled or challenged. It is harder to reverse a bad pattern of behaviour than to stop it developing in the first place.

The Art Of Control

Most humans and dog owners share the flaw of inconsistency. Depending on our mood, we may allow a dog to do something one day that we will reprimand it for the next. Dogs do not understand inconsistency in quite the way that we do. To them it can signify a 'leader' who is not unassailably in charge. So the first rule of Collie control is to make yourself consistent in all interactions and commands involving your dog, however hard this will seem at times. It will pay dividends.

Your dog should never be allowed to bustle ahead past you through gates or doors on or off the lead, nor be allowed to wander vast distances away from you when you are on walks. From very early on, encourage the Collie puppy to wait each time you go through a doorway, and to come back to you when called.

Training, 'Disobedience' and the Collie Mind

Before we look at individual commands or 'tasks' you can teach your Collie, it is important to understand that successful training, in all areas, will revolve around how well, or not, you can 'tune in' to the mentality of the dog you are taking on as your 'pupil'.

Because Collies are often witnessed doing very 'clever' things, in work or competition, a popular myth has arisen that they are 'very easy to train'. This isn't, however, strictly true.

Collies are basically very *quick learners* - which can sometimes actually be a vice as well as a virtue as far as training is concerned. This is because they can rapidly start to 'second guess' or 'over-anticipate' commands you may be about to give them, or - even worse - learn 'bad' habits or 'wrong' responses/reactions just as quickly, and effectively, as they can learn 'good' or more preferable ones.

It is incredibly easy, for instance, to 'teach' a Collie to be 'disobedient'. All you need to do is give your dog far more fuss and attention - in terms of wheedling, pleading, shouting, etc - when it doesn't comply quickly with your wishes, and by contrast take its better behaviour or more 'obedient' reactions virtually for granted. To avoid this occuring you must *always* praise your Collie profusely the *instant* it does something right, and make any other less desirable responses unrewarding - if only because you offer them comparatively little attention or credit.

Most Collies respond well to calm , clear and authoritative commands, but their natural sensitivity means they can get easily stressed or demoralised when shouted at or 'bullied' in any way - either physically or verbally. If you do badly lose your temper, or become abusive in any way towards your collie during training, or while attempting to teach it a particular command, it can have some pretty dire consequences.

To think and perform at their best, Collies need to have both confidence in themselves and a lot of trust invested in their owners or handlers. If you ever start to undermine these vital things, through being harsh, impatient or at all 'persecutory' in the way you train your Collie, you could end up with a dog who will no longer respond so well or readily to you. You might think, in such a situation, that you have a dog becoming 'more and more disobedient', when in truth it has simply become totally inhibited by a fear of failure - or principally the anger and disapproval with which its 'failure' seems to be met with by you. In short, it no longer wants to try to do what you ask for fear of the consequences of getting it 'wrong'.

Training all dogs takes tremendous patience - but also great leeway, on the owner's behalf, to let a dog get things 'wrong' without any 'threat' or unpleasant consequence being attached to 'failure'. This way its confidence in itself and its trust in you will be maintained - and also its motivation to keep on trying until it eventually gets something right.

And as long as you are patient, make commands very clear, and keep training sessions short and highly enjoyable (with the use of toys, games, treats, and loads of praise when appropriate), rather than some tedious or oppressively administered chore, rest assured that your Collie *will* eventually get things right for you in the end.

Meanwhile if you do ever badly lose your temper with your Collie during training, here are some immediate 'damage limitation' measures you should employ:

- **Make an excessive fuss of the dog by way of an instant 'apology' - the quicker you do this, after any assault on its confidence, trust or pride, the better. Collies really do appreciate the significance of such a gesture, if the timing is right.**

- **Rapidly lighten your mood and get out a toy for the dog that you can play with together.**

- **Have fun with the dog and continue to praise it and make a fuss of it.**

- **Sit your dog down gently and ask it to stay while you walk away. Then call it to you enthusiastically. The quicker and more eager its response to come to you, without deviating or stalling apprehensively, the more likely it is to have 'forgiven' you and regained its confidence.**

- **If it does noticeably deviate or stall, then you will have to work harder to regain its trust and confidence. Praise it excessively for the slightest sign of**

cooperation towards your requests, engage it enthusiastically back into enjoyable shared play, and make future training a lot less pressurised or confrontational.

Do note, however, that the above can only work to the best effect if you rarely are harsh on your dog in training, or if you have never lost your temper with it before. You cannot simply fall into a constant pattern of being harsh on your dog, then suddenly asking it to 'trust' you again, without filling it with lingering insecurities and doubts - neither of which are going to aid your success in training it, long-term.

Never forget that Collies are highly sensitive and intuitive dogs whose spirits are easily crushed by harsh and heavy-handed treatment. Constantly shouting at, or hitting your dog does not make it respect you. It just makes it insecure and afraid. Neither does it make you a good 'pack leader'. It just makes you a bully who cannot communicate with your dog in any more intelligent or effective way.

These considerations apart, some Collies can seem 'disobedient' or 'unresponsive' when they are merely stressed - see Chapter 7 - and therefore cannot concentrate well, or because for some reason they lack suitable faith in, or respect for, their owner's authority. In the latter case, a good dog trainer - and particularly one with much experience of Collies - should be able to help you overcome this hurdle, as well as outline some better overall methods of teaching and control.

Now let us look at some specific - and basic - training 'tasks'.

Recall

Many owners who experience difficulty with the 'recall' command do so for a variety of reasons. First, they do not teach it early enough. If you cannot make your puppy come back to you on command in the home environment, your chances of managing it in the park, when the dog is older and far more distracted by other dogs, exciting smells etc., are pretty slim.

Second, because constantly chasing after your dog is tiring, and few people like standing in a park shouting at a dog that is blatantly ignoring them, owners let a pattern get established whereby the dog runs off, does what it wants to do and only comes back when it feels like it. This suits the dog fine, but does not signify an owner in control.

Third, it is easy to get annoyed and frustrated when your dog runs off and takes an age to come back. But if you fall into the trap of shouting or, as sadly can be often witnessed, hitting it, you are effectively punishing it for coming back. It is therefore even less likely to be in a hurry to get back to you next time.

Fourth, as owners, we can consistently overlook what a boring, unappealing or 'too readily available' option we can pose for dogs to come back to when out. Dogs see us round the clock, every day. There's nothing remotely novel or compelling about our company, in itself, to them, compared to all the other exciting distractions that face them in the context of a trip out. So we have to give them some *reasons* why coming back to us fast, when we're out, might be a good idea.

How many owners, when out, only call their dogs back to them to put on the lead and take home? So why would a dog want to hurry back to you in this situation, once it has realised that a 'recall' means the end of freedom and fun? If owners, instead, routinely called their dogs back to them when out, just to praise them, or give them a treat, or play an exciting game with them before sending them back off again to continue enjoying their freedom, what a difference this might make to better recalls.

Many owners also easily fall into the trap of 'waiting at their dogs pleasure' when out. They'll hang patiently around, waiting for their dogs to finish smelling things/playing with other dogs etc. If the dog thinks you will always be waiting around for it while it does what it likes, where is the incentive to come back to you in a hurry? So instead, when you decide it's time to go, you go - quickly with the appearance of urgency. It's then up to the dog to always be worrying about where *you* are, rather than the other way around.

The key to good recalls are:

1. **Starting young** and getting a set idea into your dog's mind that coming to you will always be the most pleasant and rewarding option, because there will always be treat or game or praise in the offing.

2. Never letting your dog get too far away and out of control in the first place.
The latter might sound simplistic, but most dog owners find there is a critical dis tance within which their dog will still listen to them and come back when called. It can be up to 20 metres or more, depending on the individual dog. Beyond that, they seem to go 'deaf' to all commands. For maximum control, it obviously makes sense to keep your Collie within that critical distance when out walking.

3. Be a more interesting and 'important' companion to your dog when out. In other words, give it real reasons why coming back to you quickly will always be a good, rewarding or 'sensible' idea.

Recall, together with 'down', 'stay', and 'leave!' (as in leave that object alone) are the most vital commands you can teach your Collie in its early days. Not just to keep control of it, but also to save it from potential danger.

Down!

'Down' and 'stay' (see later) are two of the most important commands you can ever teach a Collie. Why? Well basically because the difference between an owner whose Collie has been taught reliably to go down and stay down, instantly, on command and one without this asset is much like the difference between a driver whose car has steering and brakes and one whose car has neither.

Think about it. If you have a dog taught to immediately go down and stay where it is until told to do otherwise, then you can not only prevent it from getting into danger - e.g. running on to busy roads - but you also have the ability to instantly halt any form of behaviour in the dog which is undesirable, such as chasing, and then redirect its attention back to you.

As quickly going down on to the ground can be a natural part of normal working - or 'stalking' - behaviour in Collies, teaching them a command that accompanies this action shouldn't be too hard.

In the early days, each time you see your dog actually going fully down - rather than just crouching - accompany this action as it happens with the word 'down!' Then reward the dog with much praise. Another way to get your dog to learn to go down is to hold a treat under its nose while it is sitting, then lower this gradually to the floor so the dog has to sink down into a lying position to get it. Once your dog learns what your command 'down' means, praise it well each time it correctly responds. Then get into the habit of only giving it a treat or praising it heavily when it responds *quickly*.

It is also a good idea to accompany the word 'down' with a hand signal - such as sweeping your arm palm downwards to the ground. This will make the command much clearer at distance, or in later years when your dog's hearing might not be so good.

Stay!

Most Collies pick this up fairly quickly. It is often best to proceed on to this command from 'down', when the dog is less likely to quickly and automatically follow after you. There is no point in using the word 'stay' when the dog is obviously moving. Wait until you have moved a few paces back from your dog and it has stayed still before using the 'stay' command. Again, you can back it up with a hand signal, such as an outstretched arm with palm outwards. But do not stick your hand right over the dog's head as this can appear quite threatening from its line of vision.

Start with very small distances with the dog staying, then work up to greater ones. But always make sure you go back to the dog, while it is still staying, to reward it. It should not, when it feels like it, break its stay to come to you. 'Stay' should mean stay in its mind, up to the point where you tell it it can do something else. But it is unkind to make your dog stay too long in one position.

'Stay' and 'down', together with 'recall' are something you should be practising all the time with your growing Collie, but not to the point where the dog's enthusiasm and motivation start to wane through over-training. Training sessions should be kept short and made fun, and ended with a game or a good walk. They shouldn't be stultifying and oppressive procedures that your dog begins to dread.

Leave!

The 'leave' command is a vital one to employ should your dog look in danger of biting, eating or picking up something it shouldn't. One way to work at it is to place an empty food bowl on the ground and walk your dog up to it on the lead. As soon as it looks down at the bowl, encourage it to look up at you instead. Say 'leave' and, when it does, reward it with a treat it particularly likes, saying 'leave' at the same time. Encourage the dog to walk away with you with a call of 'come'. Make sure it is coming with you of its own choice, and not being pulled away on the lead. As it comes with you quickly reward it again.

The next step is to put some only moderately exciting food in the bowl, e.g. carrots, and repeat the exercise. Initially what you have in your hand as a reward should always be tastier and more rewarding than what is in the bowl. As the dog's conditioning to leave and come with you gets stronger and stronger, you should be able to put really tasty food in the bowl and still have the dog leave and follow on command.

Dog trainers at local classes may help you work on all these commands and offer additional advice. You will want to be working at faster and faster responses to commands. Often this is done by only rewarding the dog for the quickest, rather than just any, response to a command.

Reinforcement

Throughout early training, understand the principles and importance of continued 'positive re-inforcement'. In other words, each time you ask your Collie to do something, and it gets an instant reward - be it a treat, toy or lavish praise - for performing this action, it will be motivated to repeat such rewarding behaviour. In time, with enough consistent and immediate rewarding of 'good' or 'preferred' behaviour actions, the dog will be doing what you want it to through willing choice, rather than being pressurised by coercion.

Anticipation and Control

Much of good control in Collies is about anticipation; understanding the stimuli that are likely to trigger its energetic instincts. With experience and good observation, you will soon get to know when your dog's 'chase', 'herd' or 'grip' instincts are about to be activated. If circumstances make them inappropriate, then this is the time you step in and take control. Do this either by checking the dog with commands like 'down' or 'stay', or by giving it something else better to do. If the dog stops a chase and lies down on your command, make sure it understands that it is the 'down' you are rewarding and not the chase.

Because much of what Collies do, and how they react, is instinctive rather than learned or conscious choice, the urge to react and do as they do does not necessarily diminish in time with regular checking. If their instincts are relentless, then so must be your level of anticipation and control. But be aware that in return for your dog's 'checked' co-operation in circumstances where its instincts are inappropriate, you must in turn allow other outlets for its exceptional energy. Otherwise you will end up with one very frustrated dog.

You may also have to learn how to properly 'command' your dog with sufficient authority. It does not come naturally to some less assertive characters. It often baffles owners in dog training classes that a dog will obey the dog trainer first time on a command that they have been practising to little effect for five minutes. This is not just some 'magic skill'. It is because the dog trainer knows how to put a real note of authority in his or her verbal command, and this is something you may feel you need to practice.

When you are looking for training classes for your growing dog, be aware that some will be better than others. Some may be too big, or contain one or two really 'disruptive' dogs which will affect the learning abilities and concentration of all the others. Some may practice 'punishment' methods which you may rightly not like the look of. If you walk into any class that advocates indiscriminate shaking of Collies off the ground by the scruff of their necks to gain subservience, please go elsewhere. We are supposed to have left the Dark Ages. This is no way to treat an intelligent and sensitive dog. It can also be a very dangerous way to treat one, in terms of potential canine retaliation, if you lack experience of the breed. Shop around until you find a class, or trainer, that best suits you and your Collie.

Growing Pains

Apart from early training, there will be other issues to bear in mind as a Collie reaches adolescence. You may need to change its diet to cope with the demands of growth and increased energy output, but do so with caution.

In recent years, research by veterinary experts has come to the conclusion that diets promoting excessive growth in young dogs over a short period of time can have an impact on developing skeletons which might not always be beneficial. It potentially exacerbates joint conditions like hip dysplasia and another disorder called OCD (osteochondritis dissicans) which commonly affects elbows and shoulders. For fuller details see Chapter 9 on *Collie Health.*

Many leading food manufacturers are now well aware of this risk and have adapted diets for growing dogs accordingly. But it is still something you may want to research fully - perhaps with help from your vet or a recommended animal nutritionist - before deciding on the best diet for your growing Collie, as both hip dysplasia and OCD are no longer uncommon in this breed.

Signs of HD and OCD are usually first apparent in adolescent Collies, particularly after demanding exercise when a noticeable lameness and distinct discomfort in either back or front legs is apparent. Both conditions have a hereditary factor and, diet apart, can be worsened by too much exercise when the dog is still young enough for its bones not to be properly formed. For this reason, it is often advised to restrict your puppy to lead exercise only until it is at least six months old. Excessive trauma to any young dog's joints can store up bigger problems for later life, including arthritis.

A Question Of Sex

Obviously as Collies enter adolescence they also progress on to sexual maturity, typically between six to twelve months. In dogs this can mean the onset of classic 'male behaviour' like leg-cocking and territorial 'scent-marking' when urinating, and bitches will experience their first 'heats'. Nature has made canines highly adept at finding mates when the urge and opportunities arise, and the number of Collie crosses currently at large on the planet will give you some idea of how successfully they spread their genes with or without the owner's knowledge. When driven by the urge to breed, natural Collie intelligence and agility can turn them into escape artists in the Houdini class.

Whether or not to spay or neuter your dog, or whether or not to breed from it are questions that divide and test many owners. But you have to make a decision based on practicality and not sentiment. If every pet owner who thought that their dog was an exceptional specimen bred from it, the streets would be knee-deep in their surplus offspring.

When you keep a dog entire, it will be prone to wandering after bitches, suffering regular agitated bouts of sexual frustration and have higher levels of aggression, particularly to other male dogs. In later life it will suffer a far greater risk of prostate and testicular cancer and other hormonally triggered health problems.

When you keep a bitch entire, not only will you have to endure the regular worry and inconvenience of heats and potential 'accidental pregnancies' without hawk-like supervision, but there will also be greater associated health risks in later life. These include mammary tumours, which can ultimately be fatal, and a potentially life-threatening condition called pyometra. Pyometra is a womb infection that usually occurs six to eight weeks after a heat and almost invariably necessitates a complete hysterectomy (removal of womb and ovaries) to save the bitch's life.

Contrary to sentimental myth, dogs do not miss what they have never had, e.g. litters of puppies, or realise they no longer have what they used to have, i.e. certain reproductive organs. It is humans, not dogs, who tend to agonise most over the whole neutering and spaying business. Dogs do not lengthily philosophise, they just get on with life, which is one of their greatest charms.

As someone all too conscious of the number of unwanted Collies there already are desperate for homes, I find it hard to recommend anyone breeding any more through irresponsibility or misplaced sentiment. Would you be able to chart a full genetic history - in terms of temperament and health disorders - of both parents of your planned pups? Would you know how to see a bitch through a difficult birth and how to raise healthy pups? Breeding is not a task for the unknowledgeable and unprepared.

Once you have come to a decision to spay your bitch or neuter your dog, the next consideration will be the optimum time to do it. Vets can vary greatly in their opinions about this. Some vets will recommend neutering dogs at around six months, before hormonally induced patterns of behaviour become too mentally ingrained. Some will prefer to do it later, after hormones have played their part in the full development of the male dog's adult physique. Others, of course, may tell you not to do it at all unless your dog's hormones are making it particularly hellish to live with, e.g. excessive scent marking, mounting and aggression.

Some vets prefer to spay bitches before their first heat and others - again due to theories they hold about full development - would rather wait until after it. All these matters need to be weighed up, allowing you to make your decision on the basis of practicality, the best interests of your dog, and sound professional advice.

The Collie As A Family Dog

I once read an 'expert' dog book which stated: *"Border Collies, with their tendency to 'herd' children, make good family pets."* It made my hair stand on end. It made me wonder whether the author was aware of how many Collies are discarded as family pets each year because they are doing just too good a job of "herding the children".

An excited Collie chasing small children round a garden tends to be driven, unfortunately, more by the instincts of the fox in the hen run than nanny in the nursery. Small children give the dog the idea they are 'prey-sized' because they move at its eye level. The more they run and scream around, the more adrenalin rushes into the Collie's body and the more excited and determined the chase becomes.

While few Collies would ever intentionally attack a child, some get so over-aroused by the chase that, in their heightened excitement, the possibility of nipping or knocking over a youngster can arise. Part of your success in owning a Collie as a family dog will be understanding how to ensure that such chase instincts are always within your control. They must never be allowed to get out of hand. You must also constantly understand how much of what your Collie does is in response to its instincts, not because it is a 'bad dog'.

Family Status

Because of the above-mentioned problems it is not usually advisable to home Collies, particularly rescue ones, in families with small children under five. Some Collies raised with children can be doting and trouble-free angels. This can be due to expert handling by owners or because the dog has an exceptionally easy and equable temperament. We cannot all be so expert or so lucky, which is why it is still a risky venture.

If you get a Collie as a family dog then be aware that this breed has a highly developed need and feel for pack hierarchy, order and structure. It will be attuned to all the subtle shifts and nuances of individual status within the home. It may react adversely to any form of domestic turmoil or upheaval that makes it feel stressed or insecure. It may seek to establish a place in the family pack 'rankings' higher up than it should be allowed.

Often couples will say that when the 'man of the house' is away, the dog starts to 'play up' or 'take advantage of' the remaining female partner. But it is more likely that the female partner is unwittingly giving the dog the message that its status has gone up now the 'boss' is away, by allowing it sudden privileges like access to the bedroom for company or extra food treats and less rigid commands. And of course if from the dog's point of view the female partner is perceived as 'boss', the above scenario can work either way around.

How do you imagine a Collie gets the idea of who is 'boss', as far as they are concerned, in any household? It could be the person who exudes the greatest physical presence or verbal authority. It could be the person who provides the training, food, walks or toys. There are lots of interesting theories, but the dog soon makes it clear whom it most respects and pays attention to.

Unfortunately, having a Collie who thinks it only need respect one 'boss' among family members can make life pretty difficult for others in the household. So this is a belief that should not be allowed to take root. First because a dog's reinforced notion of elevated status can lead it to challenge - sometimes physically - other family members it may then consider inferior. Second, there does not seem much point in having a family dog only one member of the family can successfully handle.

A Collie's place in the family pecking order should be bottom. This does not mean the enforcement of any kind of harsh or psychologically oppressive regime. It just means sticking to some firm rules that will make a dog appreciate where it stands. Re-covering some points we have touched on earlier, these include:

The dog always eating after other family members.

The dog always following any other family member out of gates/doors.

The dog's sleeping area in a separate part of the house from the rest of the family.

Children should be encouraged to take part in all aspects of dog care, including training.

The dog never being allowed to start or win any games, or be possessive over toys, with any family member.

All family members sticking to the same consistent rules and commands.

While dogs should be taught to respect a child's commands, respect has to work both ways. Don't leave young children and dogs together unsupervised, letting the child push the dog's tolerance to the limit. It is a harrowing sight when a young child is allowed to harass a dog to sit fifty different times in five minutes without any parental reprimand. This is torment for the dog. Never allow your child to become the dog's tormentor. No good will ever come of it.

There are many families who will tell you that their Collie never gives them any problems. On closer inspection, however, you will often find that this is because the Collie is always doing exactly what it likes. The only problem with this is that the Collie will tend not to want to do anything it is told to do. (See: *Dogs Who Are Dominant, Chapter 7.)*

It is also true, of course, that some families do manage to make their Collies into a joy: obedient, fulfilled and happy. They are generally the product of good training, patience and understanding and much mutual respect established between family and dog. They are proof that when families get it right with their pet Collies, the rewards can be exceptional.

Chapter 6

COMMON COLLIE BEHAVIOURAL PROBLEMS

When we state that our dog has 'a behavioural problem' (the buzz phrase of the modern pet era), it is important to define what we actually mean. Is the behaviour really an aberrant or unusual phenomenon, or is it merely quite normal behaviour for a Collie that *we* happen to find rather inconvenient and inappropriate?

In other words, the dog's behaviour is far more of a problem for us than it is for the dog. This tends to be most likely in an overwhelming number of cases. Some may argue that when you have a Collie that is driving you up the wall with any variety of excesses, such definitions seem an unnecessary consideration. But they are important, because understanding the root cause of a dog's problem behaviour puts you in the best position to find a solution to it.

With Collies, it is particularly helpful to establish which elements of their 'problem behaviour' are due to natural in-bred working instincts, typical to the breed as a whole, and which are more specific to individual dogs. Many Collie problems can be influenced by other factors such as genetic 'faults' in temperament, and how an individual dog's behaviour becomes 'learned' as a result of the experiences it is exposed to.

The following are some common examples of behaviour owners tend to view as a problem in their dog when they are merely different ways Collies find to vent their natural personalities, working energies and instincts:

Chasing - other animals, children, bikes or cars

Nipping and herding

Over-boisterousness

Manic, obsessive and compulsive behaviour patterns - e.g. seemingly hypnotised by a moving torch beam or shadow for hours on end. Any object the dog imagines its attention can 'make move' will do.

Destructiveness and barking. Both are often ways in which a dog with a high need for physical and mental exercise works off its frustrations and energies should they be continually denied.

Separation Anxiety. Collies have a strong need to be part of a working 'pack'.

It is important to understand how many of the above 'problems' are due to the domestic confines we are imposing on a dog bred for a very different environment and lifestyle. You will not find many farmers, or those who keep their Collies regularly accompanied and exercised, physically and mentally, with an urgent need for a behaviourist.

While individual Collies can vary considerably, you, as a pet Collie owner, will obviously want to know how the problems produced by their working instincts can best be dealt with in the home. The easiest answer would be to tell you not to let such patterns of 'instinctive' behaviour become established in the first place. But this is idealistic and of no help to those owners whose Collies' behavioural 'excesses' have already become well entrenched. So let us look at all the above problems, one by one, and consider how both prevention and cure might best be approached.

Chasing

As mentioned earlier in the book, Collies are dogs programmed to have a very rapid response to moving objects, particularly those at eye level. It may not be a very convenient response for pet dog owners, but it is a fact of life.

Once a Collie has 'locked on' to its moving target, it will want to stalk, or chase, or both, depending on how fast the object is moving, and which action it thinks will best bring the object under its control. Once the Collie has actually started chasing, adrenalin will pump through its body. The more exciting and prolonged the chase, the more 'pumped up' the dog is to get that fleeing object back under its command.

Many owners wonder why Collies persist in chasing objects they have no earthly hope of catching, such as bikes or cars. The answer is that the dog soon discovers that the chase itself can be a 'high'. And this, plus the notion that it is making cars or bikes move even faster, is enough of a reward to make the dog want to repeat the action again and again. Remember also that the dog does not *know* it will never catch that bike or car.

One has to be realistic and admit that indiscriminate chasing in a pet Collie can be very difficult to eradicate fully once its 'high reward factor' is well established in the dog's mind. But it can, in most cases, be controlled with some determined and persistent training. The first thing to do is to stop 'legitimising' your dog's chase instincts with endless ball and frisbee games. Your dog may quite rightly not understand why it is alright for it to hare after fleeing balls and frisbees but not alright to apply the same logical response to any other fleeing object. It is far better to use supreme Collie desirables like balls and frisbees very sparingly and to gain attention and control cleverly in other ways, as we shall soon see.

Once the 'legitimised' chase opportunities are curtailed, start to develop a fine anticipation of when your Collie is likely to launch into chase mode and which 'triggers' are more irresistible than others. The moment you see your Collie about to be off, get its attention. Remember at first this might not be easy. Collies can get extremely focused once they lock on to a target, and may not want to stop doing something they have done so happily and repeatedly in the past with little challenge. You must persist. Call your dog's name, throw a ball or frisbee up in the air, wave a treat, look as if you are about to run off somewhere exciting - whatever it takes to get your dog's attention. But always look as if you are about to do something fun and inviting which will be as good as, if not better than, a chase.

When you have your dog's attention, either get it to come to you and sit, or to lie down and stay, always in anticipation of a reward. If it does either on your command, give it the reward, making sure it is timed to be for the recall and obedience to the 'sit' or 'stay', and not for starting a chase. If you use a frisbee or a ball as your potential reward for such actions, always make sure you give the dog one or two runs with it before putting it away again. It is unfair, and eventually ineffective, to imply you will give a reward for a dog's attention, and then not give it when the dog complies. By keeping things like balls, frisbees or tug toys as a rare treat, you will increase their allure and therefore their attention-getting factor.

If you manage to get your dog's attention when it is about to hit 'chase mode', and also get it to do something else like come to you and sit or stay, then congratulate yourself. You are on the threshold of breaking a cycle. But you will need to keep practising. Do it again and again until your Collie becomes progressively better at breaking its chase pattern in return for doing something equally or more rewarding with you.

When you have broken a dog's chase pattern, its adrenalin levels might make it still physically geared up for that chase. For that reason, once you have distracted your dog's attention from the chase and rewarded it for other behaviour instead, it might be an idea to run through a few formal training exercises that will stretch it mentally and make it use its brain. Some heel-work, or finding a piece of food hidden in the garden, can help to reduce its excitement level. A Collie cannot employ its full mental concentration and be a mad adrenalin machine at the same time - though there are always exceptions! Do also bear in mind that running after a Collie and shouting at it to stop, once it is actually chasing, will be fruitless. Your dog will not only have got the reward of your attention for its exploits, but even better, you appear to be joining in with the fun.

Prevention of inappropriate and indiscriminate chasing should really start with pet Collies in puppyhood. The same distracting tactics apply, and likewise the limiting of 'chase' games. The earlier you start these attention re-directing techniques, the more successful you are likely to be. But do not forget that when you command a dog to stop its chase, you must give it something more rewarding to do. As the saying goes, when you give a Collie nothing to do, it turns self-employed.

Nipping and Herding

Earlier in the book we have focused on why nipping and herding can be an intrinsic part of a Collie's natural working function, but less desirable in a pet home. It is hard to think of any circumstance in the home where nipping, or 'gripping' will be anything other than undesirable. But it is important to distinguish between the instinctive nips and grips triggered in a Collie through a desire to get control of moving objects, and more serious forms of aggression, which we will cover later.

It is also important to understand how easily owners can unwittingly encourage Collie nipping by incorrect early handling and by giving the action the 'reward' of their attention. Here are some ways they do it:

1. By allowing Collie puppies to have lots of rough and tumble games on the ground with themselves or with children. These games will usually trigger much 'play biting' from the puppy which owners might consider 'harmless', given the puppy's size and baby teeth. But the dog grows up thinking such behaviour, which becomes increasingly less harmless and amusing as it gets bigger, is acceptable.

2. By letting Collie puppies have lots of tug games which they are allowed to 'win'.

3. By shouting, or even worse, running away when Collies nip. This gives them not only the reward of attention for their action, but also makes it appear that you are joining them in a 'game' and spurring their excitement on further.

When Collies take to nipping enticing objects like moving vacuum cleaners, brooms or lawnmowers, many owners find the quickest and easiest way to stop it is by putting the objects away, or only using them when the dog is not around. This is fine if you do not mind having a dirty house or a meadow instead of a lawn, but it does not solve the 'problem'.

The dog has to learn not only that you, and not it, are in charge of the moving object, but also that you are in charge of the dog's reaction to it. Most Collies are worse with such objects if they are allowed to get in front of them. From the dog's point of view biting and tugging one end of an object while you appear to be tugging and pulling the other, is very much their notion of helping a fellow 'pack' member complete a successful restraint or kill of resisting prey. The dog does it without ever necessarily realising why it does it. This is what defines an 'instinct'. Never forget how many of your sweet-faced Collie's genes date back to the wolf.

To deal with the problem of a Collie attempting to savage moving household objects you must:

1. Make the dog stay well behind you when you are using them.

2. Make the dog go down and 'stay'.

3. Reward the dog for going down and staying with a food treat or chew.

4. Keep using your moving object with the dog still staying down.

5. Reward the dog again for still staying down. Let it get up and give it more praise, only after you have put your moving objects away.

This way, your Collie will eventually get to realise that *you* control all the exciting moving objects and toys in the house. These are the sort of privileges a pack leader is supposed to have.

Initially you may find this 're-training' exercise difficult as the dog is being asked to act against its instincts. It may be frustrated at not being able to continue one of its favourite pursuits and whine or bark and refuse to stay down. Persist. Make it very clear that you are *commanding* the dog to go down and stay, not just irritably shouting at it, which will have nowhere near the same effect. Your success at this exercise will greatly depend on how much leadership control in general you have managed to establish with your Collie. It will be the same with all training exercises with them. Few Collies respond well to people who do not seem to be in charge.

Nipping

Obviously nipping people, rather than objects, is an even more serious concern. Given the modern punitive laws and social intolerance towards canine aggression, you will have to do all you can to limit occurrences of such behaviour. If you do not control it, at worst your dog's nipping behaviour could result in a court order to have the dog destroyed, and a criminal record for you.

Nipping people is a tendency that will vary from Collie to Collie and is likely to be worsened, as we have already mentioned, in dogs insufficiently deterred from doing it in puppyhood. In older dogs it has the complexity of being both instinctive and positively reinforced behaviour. The dog has gained some reward from the action sufficient enough to want to repeat it, and therefore nipping can be a very difficult thing to fully eradicate.

Nipping in Puppies

Collie puppies that jump up and nip should always be discouraged with a negative response. One way to do this is to tap the puppy firmly - but not too harshly - on the nose as it jumps and nips, or yell a loud 'ouch!' and look offended. Another method is to give it a quick squirt from a water pistol behind the ear. Whatever method you try, try to get the timing exactly right, so that the puppy makes the correct association between its nipping and the negative consequence. Your Collie needs to think that its nipping actions are bringing about the unpleasant consequences, not that you are suddenly being puzzlingly unkind to it.

Nipping in Older Dogs

You can try the same methods on older dogs, but it is much harder to make them unlearn what they have already learned is rewarding, if only because it usually triggers an excitingly animated response. Be aware that although many Collies nip as a reflex reaction to any sudden over-excitement, such as chasing or any other sudden physical stimulation or stress, it will not always be possible to predict when the triggers for such a response will occur until you have got to know your dog really well, or sufficiently well to gauge its typical reaction to a set stimulus.

Collie 'nipping' frenzies rarely occur out of the blue with no obvious trigger. Some Collies will launch an excited nip in order to control or provoke movement in any moveable person, animal or object. In others it is merely a reaction to stress (see Chapter 7 on Collie Stress for more insights on this).

Every time a Collie herds and nips something and it moves, that is one reward. If the person then tears around screaming or shouting, then that is even more fun. Which is why often the best advice you can give anyone about to be herded and nipped is to stay absolutely still and make no reaction whatsoever. No matter how much the dog 'eyes' and circles you , you do not move,or look at it.

This is about as dull and unrewarding as people get for Collies. Ingrained nippers might still have a small go at a static target, ever hopeful. But the less there is ever any reaction to such behaviour, the better the chance that it will diminish. Naturally your Collie's 'nipping targets' cannot stand still forever. But when they move the dog should not see them moving, otherwise you will be back to square one.

Instead, just as your dog looks bored to tears with its static victims, call it over to you. Make it lie down and give it a treat and praise. Then perhaps give it a go or two with that beloved ball or frisbee while your 'nipping targets' are moving and your Collie's attention is focused on you and its toy. If the dog makes any attempt to go back to its 'nipping targets' make it go down again instantly. If it does not go down instantly and is already halfway back to them, they will have to repeat the entire exercise - and so will you.

Nipping Prevention & Control

Although most nipping in Collies will be triggered, instinctively, by sudden movement or arousing animation - be this from animals, people or many other objects - unfortunately not everyone will distinguish between a dog misdirecting strong 'goading' urges on to inappropriate targets and one they imagine is 'biting' them or others because it is fundamentally aggressive or bad.

This inability for many people to see any difference between a dog compulsively responding to inborn working instiincts, and a dog who is fundamentally dangerous to them, or wishes them harm, gets an awful lot of Collies into trouble. Some may even end up being destroyed as the result of an over-zealous nipping instinct.

Nipping problems in a Collie can very quickly escalate for the following reasons:

- Because the dog wasn't sufficiently deterred from this habit when it was young

- Because the dog - through never being sufficiently deterred or prevented from nipping when very young - has learned to find this habit both fun and rewarding

- Because owners mishandle nipping scenarios - shouting at the dog, or hitting it - which can excite it or provoke it further into increased aggression

- Because the people it nips either run, shout, scream or wave their arms around, exciting the dog further, or else physically attack it - making the dog feel threatened and therefore increasingly defensive in its behaviour

We have already looked at how important it is for any possible 'target' of a Collie's nip to stay still. This is because, in Collies, chasing and nipping can often be enacted in a constant sequence, reliant on movement or animated reaction to perpetuate itself.

Now, on top of other previous advice, let us look at how else you can prevent nipping becoming too much of a problem in your Collie, and how to better control it.

First, as ever, your dog has to learn that you are in charge of its actions/reactions in any given situation. It simply must not be allowed to imagine that chasing after children, runners, bikes, or other people when out, when it feels like it, is acceptable, if only because chasing can so quickly escalate on to nipping.

Collies who have been trained to come back instantly to their owners on command, or to go down and stay down when told (see 'recall' and 'down!', last chapter) cannot chase other people or bother them. Similarly, a dog taught to focus primarily on its owner when out, and to constantly anticipate his/her next command or invitation to play an exciting game, will not be focused on any other distractions.

If you are finding it hard to get your Collie to come back to you when out, and instead it shoots off excitedly to chase other people or animals, then keep it on a long trailing line to start with (available from pet stores). Next, watch your Collie intently. The chances are you already know what stimuli will 'set it off' - e.g. runners, cyclists, excitable children or other dogs - but its body language, in terms of sudden intent gaze, lowered head and the beginnings of a stalking/crouching posture, can also signify an imminent chase/nip target ahead.

The *instant* you see this happening, get your dog's attention and focus immediately back to you, reeling it back on the line if you have to. Talk to it excitedly. Encourage it to sit for a treat or to play with a favourite toy it will only ever see when you are out and it comes back immediately to you. Have fun with your dog - make it feel it has done something really clever and pleasing to you.

Distract it long enough to pass by your dog's original chase target without incident and praise it well when it does so. Day in, day out, you must work on this excercise to the point where your Collie realises that focusing and responding to you, when out - rather than on anything else - is the most suitable, and hopefully rewarding, course of action for it to take.

If you work on this hard enough and consistently enough when out, then the time should eventually come when your Collie's attention becomes obsessively focused on you, or its toy in your hand - which is a whole lot better than having it focused on any other less appropriate targets, that's for sure.

How well the above measures will work can depend on how readily, or badly, your Collie is driven to nip someone. If you suspect it could be a real danger to others in this respect, then for its own sake, as well as the safety of others, it would be wise to take it out in a muzzle - if only to stop yourself becoming a neurotic mess of fearful anticipation, or until you feel you have got this problem under better control.

Nipping tradesmen

One reason why people such as postmen and milkmen pose such an irresistible target for Collies is that they share the familiar pattern of coming to your house and going away again. Unfortunately a dog soon gets the idea that *its* barking, chasing and/or nipping has *made* such an 'intruder' clear off the 'pack territory'. This is a fantastic ego boost for dogs and a reason why, whenever they see that postman/milkman anywhere else, or even someone in a familiar uniform, they will be highly motivated to have another 'go', backed up by the knowledge of stunning past success.

If this is really becoming a problem for you, i.e. you are getting no milk or mail, then one possible solution, depending on how amenable your past 'victims' are, is for the milkman or postman to always arrive with a treat for the dog. You can give them the dog's favourite treats. It is also an idea to make it clear to the dog that you are welcoming the delivery person. Have a chat with him or her amiably at the door if you can, and do not let your dog take the initiative by charging up and being hostile to your visitor while you are doing this.

If it is hostile, make it go inside at once and lie down. If it follows your cue and becomes more amiable, let the delivery person give it another treat and let it stay around. Once again, it is all about control and communication. You cannot just tell your Collie what it must not and cannot do. You must tell it what it ought to be doing instead. That is an abiding principle of leadership. Of course another solution is to keep your dog inside whenever such delivery people call, but this isn't always practical and doesn't solve the 'problem'.

Over-Boisterousness

This is one of the most common complaints owners of pet Collies make about their dogs. "It's mad", "it's hyperactive", "it rages round the house like a loony". Does this ring any familiar bells?

There are two things owners need to consider about this problem. First, is it really so baffling that a dog bred to have exceedingly high energy levels is being highly energetic? Second, you could unwittingly be further 'over-heating' your Collie in several ways.

Commonly this can be done through the diet you feed it. The higher the protein and fat content in a diet, the more energy it will give your dog. If many full-time working Collies can be fed diets whose protein levels range from 20% to 25%, it is obvious your pet Collie should need less. Some prepared diets are now available with protein levels as low as 14%, but these are for adult and not growing dogs. It is an idea to discuss with your vet and/or an experienced animal nutritionist what diet might best suit your dog's high energy levels in terms of one that will provide less protein but still be adequately balanced.

Collies can also get over-stimulated by too much fast and exciting physical exercise. In order to do the work that they naturally do, Collies need to be dogs with quick responses and prolonged stamina. This means dogs capable of rapidly releasing, and sustaining, high levels of adrenalin.

In their working role, not only do Collies have a chance to use up much of this adrenalin in physical effort, but they are also using their brains. In constantly moving from intense mental concentration to physical effort and back again, they are able to maintain a greater sense of balance than the pet Collie who is allowed to hare around frantically, with plenty of adrenalin but fewer constructive uses for it, and less simultaneous brainwork to keep its effects better checked.

Adrenalin is a stress hormone. It is released in all of us as a result of a sudden trauma, fright or threat. It prepares our bodies for flight or fight and sharpens all our responses. It can also be triggered by sudden strenuous exercise and /or excitement, which the brain and body can read as 'stress'. Thus, just as a Collie given no outlet for its mental and physical energy can, via ensuing frustration and boredom, be classed as 'stressed', so can one who is perpetually over-stimulated and excited.

Adrenalin is just one part of a complex hormonal/chemical reaction the body launches in response to a real or perceived threat or stress factor. It is known that such a reaction brings about many changes in the body, from raised metabolic rates to delayed muscular fatigue and altered brain function. In recent years, vets and animal behaviourists have begun to understand more fully the relationship between 'stress-loads' in animals and the effect they can have on both long and short-term behaviour.

Your dog might benefit from a change of diet, or it may require a better balanced programme of physical and mental exercise. Mental work may include 'scent tracking' games or some formal Obedience exercises, but never repeat the latter in the same predictable sequence, or over-push the dog's concentration and co-operation by making them last too long.

Living with a Collie can be like living with a highly excitable child. You will notice, however, that when such children are placed in a fairly calm environment, and given something constructive to do, there is a much higher tendency for peace to reign.

Collie Mind Games

Keeping a Collie mentally occupied at regular intervals need not always be a daunting task. Collies will often delight in being given simple problems to solve that demand initiative, and that offer some reward at the end. So, apart from the 'scent' and obedience tasks already mentioned, here are few other mind games to keep your Collie happily absorbed:

A basic activity cube, available at pet stores, or a narrow-necked transparent plastic bottle stuffed with treats such as small biscuits or grapes - which take ingenuity and persistence to remove.

A ball/favourite toy placed in a small, sealed-up cardboard box. Cut a hole in the box just big enough to allow the toy to be worked out - but not too large.

A ball put into a thick old sock, tightly knotted at both ends.

You will be able to think up more games yourself. While there is no substitute for the essential daily stimulation of exercise and training, these games can provide many a contented moment inbetween.

Compulsive Behaviour

Manic, obsessive and compulsive behaviour patterns in Collies arise, again, when an instinct is employed, in some way rewarded, and thus thereafter repeated. The object of the dog's obsession is invariably something that moves or can, in the dog's expectations or via actual physical effort, be *made* to move. Moving lights, shadows and water are common obsessions, but some Collies will even take to jumping on mats repeatedly to make the dust fly and 'move'.

It is helpful to try and recall when these obsessive, manic patterns of behaviour first started - whether it was when the dog had to be lengthily confined for some reason, or there was a climate of domestic upheaval - because often they can be a way a dog attempts to displace a feeling of stress. Through repetition, the action often becomes a habit. It also becomes a habit because the dog has learned to get a reward from it, i.e. a reduction in anxiety.

How much of a real problem such compulsive behaviour presents can vary greatly among Collie owners. Some seem to find it amusing, which tends to mean the Collie gets their full attention for doing it and is even less likely to stop it. Others will shout at their dogs to stop it, which in your dog's mind still means being extra-rewarded by your attention and seemingly excited interest, which is thus an incentive to do it again.

Lots of Collie owners think it is behaviour they can live with, bearing in mind how much else about their dog can drain their energies. It is something that can keep the dog 'occupied', which is fine so long as it isn't the *only* thing a dog has to keep it occupied. If your sole focus of physical and mental attention for seven or eight hours a day was the dust on a carpet, how sane would you emerge from this exercise a few months or years down the line?

Under-stimulation and confinement are key sources of stress in all animals, and a reason why you will see many zoo inmates displaying so-called 'stereotypical behaviour'. Whether pacing up and down in the same compulsive line, or round in circles, or chasing their tails, they are often judged to be doing so as a reaction to the stress induced by their circumstances. Stress frequently means the production of nervous energy; nervous energy means they have a need to find some action, or object,on which to displace it.

More enlightened zoos now know that the quicker they become attuned to such developing stress behaviour and find ways to help limit it by providing a more stimulating environment, the smaller the chance of such 'stereotypical' actions becoming progressively more manic and ingrained. In some cases this could literally mean to the point of insanity. The relevance all the above has for Collie owners is:

1. To make clear the link between manic behaviour patterns and stress.
2. To make owners aware that such actions will not necessarily be self-limiting.

In other words, the more the stress, and the more the dog is given little other outlets to employ its physical and mental energies, the greater the risk that manic, obsessive and compulsive behaviour patterns will not just become more ingrained, but may also get progressively worse.

If your Collie is just employing such behaviour very occasionally for short periods, and is otherwise given plenty of other outlets for its physical and mental energies, that is one thing. If such manic behavioural cycles seem to be taking over its life, that is clearly another, and not a very good indication of its psychological well-being. You will obviously have to rethink whether the extent and balance of physical and mental work you are giving the dog are sufficient for its needs. You may also have to evaluate how much of the dog's behaviour could be due to stress factors (see next chapter) which you could possibly modify or remove, or, in the case of rescue dogs, something 'learned' within a previous environment.

Obsessions & Phobias

The above considerations on 'compulsive behaviour' apart, be aware that the sensitive and highly reactive nature of the Collie's mental make-up readily dispose it, in general, towards the adoption of 'obsessions' or 'phobias' which, once acquired, can easily become deeply ingrained if not addressed by owners in time.

Most common Collie 'obsessions' - e.g. chasing cars, bikes, shadows, nipping brooms or the garden hose, rounding up or intently 'eyeing' other people or animals - revolve around the dog's compulsive need to employ its powerful inborn 'working instincts' in some way.

In the case of 'phobias', the sensitivity of the Collie temperament means these dogs can quickly develop an aversion towards, or downright fear of, any variety of objects/situations/people/noises etc. that they have perceived to be a 'threat' to themselves in some way.

If your Collie becomes gripped by some obsessive - but to you, highly inappropriate - behaviour patterns related to working instinct, or displays an obvious phobia about some object or situation, the most imporatant consideration is to try and address these forms of behaviour as *soon as they start.* If not, then they will only get worse or more compulsive through being constantly repeated.

Earlier on in this chapter under 'Chasing', for instance, we showed that the more often you let a Collie experience the 'high' of chasing things, the more it will want to chase things, and the more chasing will become a 'habit' that is harder and harder to break.

If, on the other hand, you teach your dog to go down and stay or come immediately back to you for praise and a game, *every single time* it displays the slightest sign that it is going to chase something, you stop the dog getting the rewarding 'high' of the chase, and you also start to make *not* chasing things on impulse, and instead focusing on your voice and alternative command, more of a 'habit' instead.

Most working instinct-related, obsessive behaviours of this kind in Collies follow the same lines. First there is the right stimulus or trigger, then there is the progressively more compulsive reaction that follows it. If you do not want this reaction to become progressively more compulsive and ingrained, then you have to step in and halt it before this process can occur - through giving your dog an alternative command, or something else to do, instead.

Similar principles apply to phobias. Each time your Collie is allowed to avoid the source of its fear, its fear will only get stronger, and refusing to face what it fears will soon become a pretty ingrained habit. If, on the other hand, the moment you saw that your dog was vaguely wary of something, you did not avoid it or try to soothe your dog - which invariably makes matters worse - but instead went out of your way, immediately, to look unbothered yourself and tried to get it interested in a toy or game, its original fear response might never have become so strong or firmly rooted.

Destructiveness

Destructiveness can be an ensuing result of frustration and boredom, or anxiety when you are out (see Separation Anxiety later); all are common causes of stress-related behaviour. Or it could occur simply because a dog finds such actions exciting and fun. It is certainly not a form of behaviour exclusive to Collies, but Collies are known to be more sensitive, and responsive, to the effects of anxiety and boredom than some other breeds.

Chewing and Digging

In young dogs, destructiveness such as chewing, clawing and digging up the garden is often just a part of their growing and curious exploration of the world. If you do not control this instinct early on (see Chapter 4) there is a high chance your dog will not just grow out of it.

Other, and particularly adult, forms of destruction by dogs tend nearly always to occur when owners are not present. Typically it will be the result of the anxiety and frustration a dog feels about being left on its own. What is destroyed will be determined by its particular behavioural problems. A chief target for destruction will be the obstacle, e.g. door or doorway, the dog imagines is impeding its access to you, though it may move on to other items, particularly those with the highest concentration of your scent, like shoes or bedclothes, or a certain chair. Obviously what a dog can destroy will be limited by the amount of access to different areas of the house that it has been left.

Some dogs will be more destruction-prone than others. It is not always understood why, but it is clear that the longer you leave a destruction-prone dog alone and anxious, and the more 'trashing targets' it has access to, the greater the damage it will do. Limiting a dog's anxiety about being left on its own and restricting the areas and objects it can damage in your absence will be keys to approaching the problem. Destructiveness can also be common in rescue dogs either fearful, or over-excited, by the strange new environment of your home. Increasing security and familiarity with a new environment will frequently, in time, see the destructiveness wane.

Barking

Barking is a problem quite a few owners can unwittingly encourage. In how many neighbourhoods do you see this endless cycle repeating itself: the dog barks, the owner shouts at it to shut up. Spurred on by the attention the dog's barking has got it, the dog barks again. The owner tells it to shut up again. It goes on and on, with little variation in sequence. Very soon the dog has a highly rewarding and ingrained habit.

If much of this tedium-triggered, low-key (i.e. not directed at any real alarm or threat) barking were ignored early on in a dog's life by owners, this habit would be far less likely to get rooted. We constantly forget how much of a dog's behaviour becomes consistently rewarded and reinforced as a result of the attention we pay to it.

Dogs barking in alarm in response to a perceived real threat, e.g. another dog or a ring at the door, tends to be less of a problem for most owners, as generally it is a short term response to a specific stimulus which ceases when the threat diminishes, i.e. when the other dog goes away or you open the door and welcome your guest.

If it carries on for far longer, particularly with increasing gusto, then the chances are you could have encouraged this reaction in a variety of ways. For example, you might tug harder and harder at a dog's lead/collar when it lunges and barks at a passing dog, thus increasing a sense of threat , and then shout louder and louder at it the longer and more fulsomely the dog yowls its head off. You do not have to be a canine Einstein to work out, from this, that the longer and louder you bark the better the 'back-up' and rewarding reaction you get from your owner.

Barking at the TV

Collies commonly bark because it's a boredom or tension reliever, because they are protesting at being left on their own or because they are simply excited. Many

Collies, for instance, love to bark at stimulating moving images on the television screen. My own dog had a particular penchant for football matches, wildlife documentaries and any programme featuring energetically moving animals, especially dogs. Televised sheepdog trials would be real frenzy material if I did not curb her excesses.

Obviously, much barking at the TV can be a result of excitement and frustration; the excitement of seeing things a Collie wants to chase and the frustration of not being able to get at them. But it can become extremely annoying. An automatic reaction is to shout at the dog to stop, but then you fall into the trap of encouraging the dog's excitement even further.

Do bear in mind that the dog is not trying to be annoying. It is simply acting on principles of instinct and reward. One way to curb the habit is to call the dog to you the moment it looks like launching itself at the TV screen. Make it sit or lie down, preferably with its back to the TV screen and reward it with a food treat. Make it stay down for a while and reward it with more praise. Repeat this exercise each time your dog looks as if it is about to return to a bout of TV frenzy. The timing has to be right so that the dog knows it is being rewarded for coming to you and doing what you want, not for barking at the TV. A persistent and consistent application of this exercise generally keeps the problem under control.

Barking at the Telephone

Many Collies have a similar fixation with the telephone. Much of this is due to our habit of rushing to the telephone when it rings, causing excitement. Dogs can also get anxious by the unnerving sudden changes the telephone can bring. Not only the removal of all owner attention away from the dog, but also our appearing to be excited or worried by something they cannot recognise or see.

Common behavioural advice for this problem is to get a friend to ring you regularly while you try to re-tailor the dog's responses to the phone. You do this by walking very slowly and unexcitedly to the expected call and by rewarding the dog with a food treat each time it keeps quiet. Unfortunately this will not cover you for the times you forget to go slowly and unexcitedly to the phone and do not happen to have a food treat handy.

You could also get the idea into the dog's head that you are, effectively, 'bribing' it for not doing something, rather than rewarding it for doing something else you want it to do instead. Collies are certainly smart enough to know the difference, and the message each action gives about authority. It will not take many of them long to work out that, if they go through a constant cycle of barking, then keeping quiet, then barking again, they are likely to acquire far more treats than if they just kept quiet for the duration of a phone call. They are also, simultaneously, getting extra bouts of your attention.

If only to limit this scenario, not to mention your poor friend's phone bill, another option when your dog barks at the phone is just to give it a very loud and convincing command of 'No!' and/or 'Down! Most of these commands have the same message if given in the right tone, with the right authority, especially if you have never lessened the impact of loud commands through over-use. Like many obvious-sounding solutions, this one can often be extremely effective. Remember to make full eye contact with your dog to command it to stop barking at the phone, or it will just think you're joining in.

Barking When You are Out of the House

One of the commonest problems Collie owners report are dogs that bark non-stop when the owners are out of the house. In fact, this tends to be their neighbours' problem more than theirs, but it can soon escalate into considerable ill-feeling, upset and, unfortunately, a heightened nervous intolerance to any barking at all amongst those who must endure it.

There is no mystery as to why dogs bark when their owners are out of the house; it is due to any combination of anxiety, boredom and frustration. Barking, they soon discover, displaces - and therefore relieves - such feelings, and so becomes a continually rewarding pastime as a result. The dog may also be attempting to 'call' its owners back. Since the owner eventually always does come back, to a dog's logic this is a highly effective strategy worth keeping up.

How do you stop it? First of all, try to ascertain why it has started. If the barking is part of a Collie's anxiety about solitude and separation, this has to be worked on, preferably, of course, from puppyhood onwards (see *Separation Anxiety* below). If the dog is bored and frustrated, this is usually because it has been left alone for too often, too long, devoid of company or stimulation. For Collies this is an excessive trial, guaranteed to spark some reactive outlet.

Generally, Collies cope far better with solitude and inactivity when it is introduced to them in small, gradual periods, and as part of a fixed daily routine after say, exercise, training and feeding. If you start introducing the dog to periods of inactivity and solitude while you are still in the house, with the dog resting in another room, it should learn to settle, especially if already exercised and fed. Give it a few treats and toys, and perhaps leave the radio on. You can gradually prolong the time you leave your Collie before returning, provided you only return when the dog is settled and quiet. Collies find it hard to cope with very long (i.e. over four hours) periods of solitude without any sort of stimulation, and are therefore a cruel choice of pet for people out of the house all day. If this has become unavoidable in your case, then a compromise to prevent boredom barking is to have a friend or neighbour call in on your dog and give it a quick walk, once or twice a day. That should hopefully stave off being pilloried as a Neighbour From Hell, as well as much improving your dog's state of mind.

Separation Anxiety

Separation anxiety, as we have already discussed, can be a particular problem in Collies who have a strong need to be part of a 'pack', and who find isolation particularly upsetting and threatening. It can be an especially heightened form of anxiety in dogs who have had little experience of being left on their own in puppyhood, or who for one reason or another have become overly attached to their owners.

Solitude is not a normal situation for any dog. It can be hard for many of them to appreciate not just that there are times when owners will leave them for no obvious reason, but also that when they do leave they will be coming back again. Such concerns are what lead to spirals of anxiety and all the problems that arise from the resultant stress, e.g. destructiveness, barking, manic behaviour.

Such anxiety can also be particularly acute in rescue dogs; not just because they have had one, if not more, past experiences of total abandonment by a former 'pack' but because usually, during their first weeks or months in a new home, owners will give them excessive attention. There is an understandable, though not always helpful, tendency to overcompensate for past neglect. The more attention the dog gets in an owner's presence, the more distressing a contrast the owner's absence will present.

Many dogs can be taught gradually how to accept occasional solitude. In puppyhood, this means beginning with set periods when the dog will get no attention from you while you are still in the house. Some people will advise putting a towel on a door handle or other obvious object in place to define when such periods of withdrawn attention will start and end. But some dogs will take longer to understand the significance of such things. And some dogs will soon devise ways of getting your attention that are not so easy to ignore, object or no object in place.

The crucial importance of introducing separation and solitude to Collies early in puppyhood, commonly via set times in their crate (see Chapter 4) can never be over-stressed. However, one owner of a rescue Collie I know, with acute separation anxiety problems, found a solution in this method. For a week or so she would go in and out of her front door continually, gradually building up the time she was out of the house from minutes to hours. She never paid much attention to the dog when she went out, or made much fuss of it when she came back in, but she always left the dog an item of clothing with her scent on for reassurance. Plus toys and activity cubes to keep it busy. No doubt her neighbours thought her behaviour moderately deranged, but it did work. Although she will never leave her dog on its own for long periods of time, it now happily accepts that from time to time it will have to spend a few hours on its own.

Any owner baffled by the extent of a dog's anxiety when left alone fails to appreciate the implications in the canine mind of not being with a 'pack'. A dog's innate desire to co-operate with, and conform to, the requirements of a pack do not stem from simple personal preference. They stem from an instinct to survive. Dogs have to hunt together as a pack to survive, and defend themselves, each other and their territory as a pack to survive. A dog left on its own fears instinctively for its chances of survival. To ease this fear away, you must conatantly and reinforce a notion of only temporary, and not permanent, abandonment in its mind before you go.

It can sometimes require much time and persuasion to achieve this, as you cannot expect dogs to overcome one of their strongest and most compelling natural fears overnight. It also underlines how much general stress and anxiety we can cause any dog when we force it to live a life arranged totally for human convenience, heedless of what a dog's own crucial needs and expectations might be.

There will always be times when we cannot be with our dogs. But an hour or two of occasional solitude, which the dog has been gradually taught to accept with minimal trauma, and day after endless day spent fearfully and desperately alone are two very different things. Some individual dogs cope better with solitude than others. But generally it appears to be a fact of life that most Collies cannot cope with regular and very prolonged periods of solitude, bereft of purpose, pack cohesion and leadership. And maybe we should ask ourselves how fair it is of us to expect them to.

Before moving on to the subject of Collie Stress and Aggression in the next chapter, let me stress these final points. First, Collies' lives should never be dominated by repression and disapproval. They must be allowed some freedom of action, to feel that life is good and have positive ways and regular opportunities to work off their natural physical and mental energies. Such regular enjoyable outings and experiences with your dog will not only make your dog happier and more fulfilled, and increase your bond with it, but it is also more likely to co-operate with you when you ask for a little more re-direction and restriction of its instincts in the home.

Second, never forget how much a Collie responds to praise. Keep its confidence and co-operation high by always praising it for doing something right. Don't crush its spirit by forever dealing out heavy-handed reprimands for minor misdemeanours.

Third, be conscious of the best use of rewards. When trying to shape a 'right' action or response in a dog's mind, food treats are often the quickest and most effective way of getting a message across. But once it has got the message, repeated use of them will not only reduce the dog's incentive to try harder for an even better or quicker response to your command, but it will also start to smack of bribery. You want your dog to do something because it respects you and wants to co-operate, not just because it wants a food treat. If it responds to you only when it gets a food treat, how much use is that going to be when the dog is far on the horizon or on the other side of a competition ring? Food treats are best used all the time until you get the response you require, then intermittently until you get the best response, then phased out altogether in return for praise.

Finally, should all the coverage of possible problems caused by Collie working instincts in this chapter make you feel excessively daunted, remember the good news too. There are few breeds so potentially work-driven as a Collie, but there are also very few who can match them for adaptability and a willingness to redirect their talents to other demands, given the right level of understanding and communication.

This can be seen in the way they have tackled and excelled at any number of new fields from Search and Rescue missions to helping the disabled, from Agility, Flyball and Obedience to scent-tracking expertise. This could be the reason why so many people who have made a success of pet Collie ownership can never contemplate owning any other breed. When you win the respect of a Collie's heart, it also tends to work a spell on your own.

Note: for further help, the NCDL has a wide list of advice sheets on dog behaviour. For details, see Chapter 12.

CHAPTER 7

UNDERSTANDING COLLIE AGGRESSION AND STRESS

Aggression is a phenomenon of greatest concern for dog owners. But it is also one that is routinely misjudged or misunderstood. Sometimes we can forget how much aggression, whether verbal or physical, is a regularly occurring reaction in our own lives, when we feel under pressure or threat. It is natural in human society, and equally normal in dogs.

There are many reasons why a dog has, within its own instinctive logic, a need to be aggressive: it feels threatened, it wants to protect itself, its status, its pack or its territory. The strength and rapidity of its defence may also be influenced by other factors ranging from pain and heightened vulnerability (such as when a dog is cornered or tied up) to individual genetic predisposition and existing levels of stress.

Understanding this is all very well, but we instinctively don't like aggressive dogs, nor the sight of a large predatory carnivore's teeth in full flight. It is, naturally, very scary. In asking dogs to live with us, we have put very many restrictions on what they would deem 'natural behaviour', but this does not mean that those natural instincts will ever go away. We need to realise the force and potential of such instincts when triggered. We need to appreciate how very often dealing with aggression in Collies, as in all dogs, is as much about prevention as 'cure'.

Two of the most commonly cited forms of aggression in Collies are 'nervous' or defensive aggression and 'dominance' aggression. This does not mean that Collies, as a breed, are more aggressive than any other, as every breed comprises many different individuals with very varying temperaments. It just means that in individual Collies where aggression occurs, these two forms are seen most frequently. Let us now look at them in more detail:

Nervous Aggression

Owners often consider that, in dogs, aggression is just aggression. If it all amounts to the same problems and scary scenarios, why bother to define one kind from another? The answer is a) because it is very hard to remedy a problem you do not fully understand and b) by not fully understanding it you could well make it worse.

What constitutes 'nervous aggression' in Collies? There are quite a few theories but mainly it seems to be typified by a dog who will 'shout before it is hit'. In other words, an actual threat doesn't have to materialise before the dog launches into full 'defensive attack' mode; just a quickly perceived notion of a threat can be enough.

This is often highly disconcerting for owners. It can be hard to appreciate that a dog who is launching, or threatening, a grisly attack on another dog or person may also be afraid at the same time, or that fear and insecurity are often at the root of such actions. If Collies are 'fearful' dogs, then we need to ask why they have become this way, as individuals. Frequently such over-defensive and nervous aggression can look very frightening and can appear to be launched out of the blue. But is this really the case?

Obviously a dog who feels excessively vulnerable, is in pain, highly stressed or affected by any illness or medication altering normal behaviour will be prone to more heightened defence reflexes. If the dog has a history of past abuse and harsh treatment, it may also be generally more frightened and untrusting; particularly when encountering any person/object that reminds it of such abuse and thus reactivates a sense of threat.

However, breeding factors - such as a dog too interbred, or with parents not selected for sound temperament - will also play a part. Puppies who have been poorly-handled, with a complete lack of early socialisation, will also be prone to nervous aggression. Often these factors may be found together on puppy farms and other establishments where Collie dogs and bitches are viewed as little more than puppy factories, and is a reason why a high number of Collies with extreme nervous aggression problems tend to come from such places.

As mentioned earlier, any sudden stress can also trigger a swift and instinctive defensive response in Collies, including loud commotions or bangs (such as fireworks or thunder), as Collies are particularly noise sensitive. Properly handled exposure to loud noises during puppyhood usually enables the dog to cope much better in adulthood. (Also see *'Socialisation'* in Chapter 4).

This aside, Collies as a breed are said to carry a genetic predisposition towards nervous aggression. But sometimes 'nervousness' in such dogs can also be confused with a general tendency to over-reaction or over-defensiveness under pressure, which could also have a genetic root. Collies are dogs who have been bred for centuries to possess great sensitivity and rapid responses. It is therefore not illogical to suggest that in reacting to a threat, as to many other environmental stimuli, they will have a heightened natural tendency to mentally 'jump the gun'.

It is important to keep Collie 'nervous/defensive' aggression in a proper perspective, in terms of the low percentage of dogs in whom it can be regarded as a really serious problem, unresponsive to any remedial therapy. The most vital aspect about such aggression is the need to recognise it in its early stages, and handle it in a way that will not make it worse. Although there are, to the trained eye, some classic signs in a 'nervous defensive' dog, e.g. ears back, a half-retreating posture, it is really best to get some expert behavioural advice if you are not sure; advice not just on how to spot it, but also how to best deal with it in an individual dog. Let me stress here the word 'expert', which means you should seek out a person who really knows about such aggression in *Collies,* as opposed to possessing just generalised canine knowledge, and has a recognised measure of success with past cases; in other words, cases that could be improved or controlled enough to make for a happier and better-balanced dog.

To give you some idea of the tragedies that can occur when people seek advice for this problem from self-considered 'experts' who clearly aren't, look no further than the case history of a young bitch rescued by The Border Collie Trust of Great Britain.

Jennie Booth, who runs the BCT (much more on Rescue in Chapter 8) remembers how this bitch "originally started off with just a common wary puppy's 'food possession' problem, which could have been solved there and then with some sensible remedial training." (Typically this can be done by owners making their presence always a 'welcome sight' at the dog's food bowl. Beginning with an empty dish in front of the dog, owners can, bit by bit, put small portions of food or other treats into it. Eventually the dog should realise that no food or treats will be forthcoming if it is snappy or ill-mannered and that you are there to put food into that dish, not take it away.)

However, as Jennie continues; "the owner of this dog said he was not going to put up with her growling at him, so he went to get some 'expert' advice. The advice he got was this: Next time the dog growled at him he was to pick her up by the scruff of the neck and shake her till she wet herself in fear. Then he should fling her on her bed and give her a good thrashing. And he did all this. Repeatedly. Can you imagine anything more cruel and mentally damaging for a young dog?"

Anyone who meets 'nervous/defensive' aggression in a Collie with retaliatory aggression or abuse themselves is generally looking at a recipe for disaster. Instead of taking away reasons why the dog should need to be so defensive and afraid, you are just giving it reasons why it should. In order to feel less afraid a dog has also got to trust its owner. You would not believe the word of someone who had beaten you, and always betrayed you when you were fearful, that the world is a safe place. Neither would a nervous dog.

Much remedial therapy for 'nervous/defensive' Collies revolves around building up a trust. Often its fear/defensive reactions, where possible, are met with indifference, rather than the sort of excessive sympathy and soothing that might inadvertently tell the dog it is right to be afraid. A general down-playing of the dog's fearful/defensive behaviour, by ignoring it, or strolling nonchalantly off to play with something that makes the dog's mood shift from fear to curiosity, is basically giving it the cue that what it is doing is both unnecessary and inappropriate. But the dog has to come to this decision for itself in its own time. It should never be pressurised to come out of corners or drop defensive postures, as this may reverse any progress.

A general reduction of stress and the use of special 'calming signals' (see later section on stress) should also help. It should never be forgotten what intrinsically sensitive dogs Collies are. This is why they can offer such unique qualities to people who respect and understand them, and so easily be destroyed by those who don't.

Dogs Who are Dominant and Stress-Related Aggression

Just as some Collies can be exceptionally sensitive and/or nervous dogs, others can be quite dominant, especially when afforded enough opportunity. In chapter one we looked at how a certain dominance of personality or forcefulness of character aided a Collie in its traditional working role, enabling it to shift and goad on stubborn livestock bigger than itself. Such character leanings do not always go down so well within the family home. Problems with dominance and dominance aggression are more commonly seen in male dogs. And extremely nice people often own them.

Lots of people live with dogs who are dominant and might not even know it. What they might know is that they have a dog which suits itself about where it goes in the house and where it sleeps. It demands to be fed when it feels like it, runs off with toys it believes are its own, seeks attention when it suits it and shuns it when it doesn't.

The dog doesn't seem to be that much of a 'problem'. And why should it be as long as it is doing what it wants and appears to be running the place? You might just find, however, that it doesn't want to do anything you tell it to do. And when you try to move it off 'its' chair or take away 'its' toys, there could be a hint of aggression in the air.

It can be very dangerous to push a dog with a high sense of status into a challenging confrontation. Instead you have to work on its notion of how superior it really is. In Chapter 5 we looked at ways to achieve this in growing dogs. Much the same principles of 'status demotion' apply in adult dogs, but they can take much more time and persistence to be effective - see next section on 'Leadership'.

One also has to be realistic and say that some people, particularly if not very forceful characters themselves, can be quite intimidated by a dominant dog. Many don't actually like to admit that they have one and will skirt around the issue. They will say the dog is just 'disobedient' or 'bolshie'.

Some might conclude that it's easier to let the dog do what it wants to do to avoid hassle. Most of us know such people. Their dogs always seem to be as much of a problem to other dogs and people as they are to their owners. It is no fun owning a dog like this.

Owners struggling to get the upper hand with dogs who are dominant can often be tempted to 'send it away for some training to sort it out.' This can be a disaster. How well do you really know the trainer you are sending your dog off to? How do you know that he or she won't use punishment methods or other brutal training techniques that will render the dog highly fearful, and therefore potentially far more dangerous, when it comes back?

You cannot just send problem dogs to trainers like faulty watches to the menders and expect that to be the end of your worries. The trainer has not got to live with your dog, nor the consequences of any training that backfires. But *you* have to. Most good dog trainers will insist that any 'remedial training' is undertaken with owners present and participating, and will not use unkind methods. Remember it doesn't take any skill to make a dog afraid, and a dominant dog exchanged for a frightened one is hardly solving your problems.

Being a Leader

A Collie's strong sense of pack hierarchy can often lie at the heart of many dominance-related problems. It is a sense that gives them an unerring ability to detect any sign of 'weakness' in the household 'chain of command'. Every time we allow a Collie to 'dictate the agenda' for anything that happens in our home - e.g. when it is fed/walked/petted/given treats or played with - we can put confusion in the dog's mind as to who is really 'in charge' of its pack.

Some Collies can feel compelled to take advantage of this ambiguous state of affairs, either through developing a series of manipulative ploys - e.g. whining, barking, or other forms of 'pestering' to get what they want from you, be it food, a game or simply attention. Others of a more dominant frame of mind may feel tempted to physically challenge owners who lack sufficient authority in their eyes.

It is easier than you might think to give your Collie the 'wrong' message about your true level of authority. Every time you give your dog 'something for nothing', i.e. treats or toys when it has done nothing in return for you, or fuss over it for no reason, or let it charge past you through doorways or up the stairs, or allow it access to 'privileged' territory, like beds or furniture, you can inadvertently tell it that it is more 'important' than it really should be.

If you suspect your dog could be having far too much of its 'own way' in your house, and that this, in turn, is giving you problems with its behaviour - e.g. its level of obedience or its tendency to 'challenge' you physically - then this is what you must do:

Never give your dog any unearned attention. When you come home, for instance, ignore the dog totally for a good five minutes, no matter how much it seeks to get your attention. Then call the dog to you and greet or stroke it as normal.

Get into the habit of always calling your dog to you to get attention - do not let it ever get attention from you on demand, or through any form of 'pestering'. If it does 'pester' you in any way, simply ignore it until it settles down again.

Do not give your dog treats - *ever* - apart from as a reward for training

Your dog *must* be taught to obey the command to *immediately* lie down and stay down, exactly where you tell it to, until you allow it to move again. This command will not only consistently convey to your dog that you have authority over its actions - it is also a very handy one to use whenever your dog is doing something you do not want it to do

If you want a game with your dog, you start it when you want to and end it when you want to. The same with walks and mealtimes - all these things happen only when you decide. If your dog ever tries to 'pressurise' you into going for a walk, or having a game, totally ignore it until it settles down again.

Keep the dog off all the furniture and out of the bedrooms. If your dog has ever 'challenged' people at the top of the stairs, then make it stay downstairs in future, with the aid of a special child gate if necessary.

These are just some basic strategies that can help to revise a dog's notion of its own 'status' in relation to yourself or other household members. They can take much persistence and steely resolve to enforce consistently, but the more relentlessly you do this the more progress you should see.

Sometimes, with excessively dominant male dogs, castration might be recommended. This can have varying degrees of success, depending at what age it is done, and how much of the dog's dominant behaviour has become mentally ingrained through repetition, rather than fuelled by hormonal surges. It is something you may wish to discuss with your vet, together with a possible change of diet. Diets lower in fat and protein often make for a far less 'heated' dog.

Collie Stress

We know what happens to us when we feel stressed. We feel fidgety and edgy. We may find it hard to think straight or concentrate on simple mental tasks that have no relevance to the source of our anxiety. We may generally over-react to remarks and gestures that normally would cause no sense of threat or irritation. Our stomachs may be churning. Metabolic changes and reactions in the body, whether or not we realise it, are making us behave in such a way. The body's reaction to stress, i.e. faster circulation, surges of energy, sharpened defensive responses, is a function required for survival in all animals. Somehow we don't always see it in dogs as readily as we see it in ourselves.

Given a Collie's notorious sensitivity, and capacity for highly tuned responses, it is not hard to imagine why this breed can be especially vulnerable and reactive to stress and its mental and physical side-effects. Some people can be similarly inclined. The medical world has now defined the 'Type A' personality. They are often typified as living on their nerves, being always 'on the go', highly motivated and in terms of defensive responses, being 'on a short fuse'. Many Collie owners might see parallels between such people and their dogs.

When Collies are described as 'mad' or 'behaving weirdly' by their owners, it is necessary to find out to what extent stress could be the underlying cause, and also consider what could possibly be done about it. A stressed Collie might have any or all of the following symptoms:

It will be restless and over-active.

It will not be able to concentrate on mental tasks or training commands.

It will be excessively over-reactive/defensive/destructive.

It will scratch, lick or bite itself.

It will lose its appetite/lose weight.

It will shake or shiver.

It will bark or whine without any real reason.

It will become obsessed with seemingly pointless, repetitive tasks (e.g. tail-chasing).

It will be less healthy, e.g. poor coat, diarrhoea, itchy skin.

Although the reasons for such stress behaviour or symptoms may not be immediately obvious, some common triggers include:

Domestic upheaval, e.g. new baby, a move, family illness or strife, any other unsettling shift in the usual 'pack' or hierarchical status-quo.

Too little physical exercise, or too much of the over-stimulating/exciting kind.

General harassment, e.g. from children, or because the dog has no peace or respected retreat area when it needs it.

Hostility or aggression from owners or other dogs.

Physical discomfort, e.g. pain, illness, injury, thirst, hunger, heat or not being able to relieve itself when it needs to.

Too many demands/ too much pressure put upon it , e.g. over-training, too little freedom of action, too many harsh or oppressive commands and restrictions on behaviour.

Confinement and separation anxiety.

Sexual frustration/hormonal disruption.

Loud noises or other frightening/threatening stimuli.

It would be impossible for any of us, let alone our dogs, to live in a world totally devoid of stress factors. But the above list might make us aware of how many of the things that cause stress to dogs can be instigated and controlled by us. Therefore they are factors that we can change or modify.

It is also important to understand how much the restrictions and pressures of modern living bring us all under forms of stress which our bodies were not originally designed to cope with. Traffic jams, job pressures, money worries, or even noisy neighbours can all influence our perception of personal security; our ability to feel in charge, or generally cope with life.

Now consider the average dog's life. They have the same fundamental need for personal security. They are also animals for whom an inability to escape or control their living environment is an every-day reality of existence, as long as they remain in human ownership.

A dog's perception of how inherently 'safe' it feels in your ownership, or under your 'leadership', will obviously have bearings on its stress levels. Depending on the individual dog's character or past life experiences, some may take longer to achieve this sense of 'safeness' in your hands than others. Here are some ways we can help to establish a sense of security in a dog:

Give it a set, reassuring daily routine of things like walks, meals, grooming, 'toilet opportunities'.

Share lots of fun and enjoyable experiences together.

Don't shout at or punish your dog for reasons it fails to understand - which means things that have happened even minutes earlier - or shout at it or physically punish it generally. Firm and consistent commands, together with much praise when the dog does something right, will do far more to build its self-confidence and respect for you.

Limit excessive training demands until the dog feels sufficiently confident in you and itself; remember, a stressed dog can find it very difficult to concentrate.

Try to limit the occasions where the dog gets harassed or generally over-excited by children or anyone else.

Phase in solitude and separation very gradually (see previous chapter) and limit any continually long periods when the dog is left alone and anxious.
Be alert to your dog's mood and overall health; any suspicions about illness or developing ailments should be checked out.

Don't leave the dog in situations where it feels threatened and defenceless,

e.g. tied up somewhere where it might be tormented by children or frightened by loud noises and unable to escape; all made worse by the sense that it has been banished from your protection.

Ensure that the dog always has a safe refuge or corner it can retreat to in total peace when it needs to.

Calming Signals

Over and above such considerations, one could try some of the 'Calming Signals' developed by a Norwegian canine behaviourist, Turid Rugaas, to help reduce stress and anxiety. Some time ago, Turid discovered that dogs actually have their own 'language' for defusing conflict and minimising tension in each other. She believes that humans can learn to use these 'Calming Signals' on their dogs in much the same way. Here are just some examples of them.

To promote greater calmness and minimise the need for confrontation in another dog, or their owner, canines will typically, according to Turid:

Avert threatening eye contact by turning their heads or whole bodies sideways

Yawn or lick their noses

Wag their tails

Sniff the ground

Sit down, perhaps with backs turned, or lie down with belly to the ground

Adopt a 'play bow' position with legs splayed out and down in front and bottoms in the air

Obviously some of these will be harder for humans to recreate than others. But averted eye contact, sideways postures, licking and yawning, sitting and lying, and stretching arms down to suggest a 'play bow' position can do much to pacify stressed or troubled dogs as part of a general tension and anxiety reducing programme.

In recent years, Turid Rugaas's 'Calming Signal' methods have been used with much success on such dogs throughout the world. For more information on her work, training camps and international seminars, see *Further Advice* in Chapter 12.

In concluding our chapter on aggression and stress in Collies, let us not forget how often they can be linked together, and how much we can do to prevent extremes of either. We will never live in a world where all Collies and their owners live lives of untroubled harmony, but what we can do is have a dog we have learned to understand better, and manage better as a result. This might not be a perfect solution, but it is progress.

Chapter 8

THE RESCUE COLLIE

Every year thousands of Collies need new homes. Annually, The Border Collie Trust of Great Britain takes in 350 dogs alone, and has to turn away the same number through lack of space. Julie and Gary Nelder of Border Collie & Sheepdog Rescue in Lincolnshire are also one of many smaller rescue organisations continually trying to re-home unwanted dogs. Elsewhere across Britain, many of our biggest national animal charities, such as The Blue Cross, the National Canine Defence League and the R.S.P.C.A. are similarly inundated with Border Collies and Collie crosses whose owners have found them too demanding. People might conclude from such a situation that Collies are 'problem pets'. But all problems have causes, and the more one looks into the background of many Collies who end up in rescue centres, the more one realises how many of them have been human-made.

Bad Breeding

We have already looked in depth at how a Collie's natural working instincts can cause problems in the domestic environment if the dogs are not properly handled. And obviously they are unlikely to be properly handled if they are not first properly understood. What we have not dwelt on so thoroughly until now is the issue of bad breeding. Bad breeding takes us into the darker, more depressing world of Collie existence; the farmyards and the puppy farms where these dogs can be produced and sold like a cash crop to the first available bidder with the right money in their hands. Some pedigree breeders will also be less conscientious than others. A bad breeder is someone who continually puts financial gain above the long-term welfare of their dogs, and who is happy to make the results of such an irresponsible policy somebody else's problem. In other words, some naive new owner, or an over-worked rescue centre, has to deal with the consequences of a problem they have made.

Whether you are considering getting a rescue Collie or a Collie puppy, you must be aware of how such a badly -bred background can influence its future suitability as a healthy and well-adjusted pet. First, it may have genetic disadvantages, in terms of physical and temperamental soundness. Dogs that are mass or non-selectively bred, especially with no thought given to genetic unsuitability or incestuous links, are destined to produce inferior offspring.

Second, vital early socialisation will be lacking. A puppy likely to have been conceived in a barn, born in a barn and spent most of its early weeks there in isolation and/or darkness, or holed up in similarly soul-less kennels, is virtually guaranteed to find future life as a domestic pet a total trial.

The longer a pup has gone through its formative weeks with no experience of other people, children, animals and the general everyday bustle of the world outside, the greater its chances of being totally traumatised by stress and fear when those experiences finally arrive. And as we know by now, fear and stress in Collies never mean good news.

It is a fact of life that any breeder, good or bad, and whether they specialise in working dogs, pedigree dogs or dogs destined for the pet market, will always have surplus puppies on their hands at some time. But there is a world of difference between a well-bred and conscientiously-raised surplus puppy going to a suitably vetted home and a surplus puppy with none of these advantages on sale to the first bidder at the back gate.

With thought, it would not take you long to work out which of these two types of puppy will be more likely to end up in a rescue centre. But you need to think about these things *before* you get your puppy, and sadly there are still not enough people who do. Which is why rescue centres remain so busy.

Hard Decisions

Working in Border Collie & Sheepdog rescue, like many breed rescues, can be exhausting and emotionally testing work. People see you as a repository for all the problems they have created, or responsibilities they have acquired, and no longer want. They want you to have them instead.

Sometimes dogs will be left tied to your back gate, abandoned by anonymous owners. Sometimes you will get calls from owners saying that unless you take on their unwanted dogs or puppies immediately they are going to be destroyed. You have to weigh up the consequences of responding to emotional blackmail, and how providing an endless outlet for unwanted dogs can only lead to the production and arrival of more.

You also have to make clear-headed and hard decisions about the future fates of the dogs you acquire. Which dogs will be suitable for re-homing as pets, which dogs are only suitable for certain homes and not others, and which dogs are too risky to re-home at all and may have to be destroyed. Visiting any Collie rescue centre, or other rescue centre where many Collies are inmates, will give you an idea of the despair caused to this breed by human irresponsibility. Dogs badly bred, dogs acquired too easily, dogs psychologically shattered by misunderstanding and abuse. It is an experience I would highly recommend to any would-be Collie owner to concentrate the mind.

Rescue workers are the people who have to try and make some sense out of all this despair. This often means having to put natural human sentiment aside in favour of what will practically be in the best interests of a dog. It is not easy work and often requires much strength of character, and knowledge of character, both human and canine. It is also not a job where you can easily switch off from fretting. As Jennie Booth of The Border Collie Trust of Great Britain is wont to say, "How's my dog? Have you rung the vet? I'll be saying that when they nail down my coffin."

But the reason why many Collie rescuers persist is not just because of their love for the breed, but because so often what they do is worth the effort. They can find troubled dogs happy new homes, they can turn failure into triumph. Maybe not quite so often as they would like, but enough to make a difference to the lives of many dogs who had no hope of another chance without them.

Rescuing Collies

The Advice at the end chapter of this book will give you details of where you might be able to rescue Collies should you want to. But before you embark on such an undertaking, bear some important points in mind. First, many of the rescue Collies you will see are more often 'farm dog' types than glamorous pedigree strains. Their looks, temperaments and backgrounds can be highly variable.

Second, it is vital to choose a rescue centre with great experience of Collies as a breed, particularly when it comes to an accurate assessment of a Collie's temperament and character. Stressed and potentially aggressive dogs matched to inexperienced or unsuspecting owners can be a recipe for disaster. This is why expert character assessment is so crucial. A really good Collie assessor will be able to give you all the bad, as well as the good, news about individual dogs and why some might be more suitable for you than others. Anyone who tells you that all their rescue Collies have no behavioural faults and are all suitable for immediate re-homing looks rather more dodgy.

Third, be aware that rescue dogs, of any breed, can take considerable time, effort, patience and commitment to properly rehabilitate. Don't get any rescue dog if you expect to overturn any existing behaviour problems overnight, or in a few weeks. Many Collies come from rescue centres with existing burdens of stress, either from previous home lives, or the anxieties of kennel life. Stress causes self-perpetuating cycles of behaviour which are not always easy to live with, but are only diminished when stress levels are diminished. Many owners underestimate how long this process can take. More on this later.

Why A Rescue Dog?

It is not hard to understand why people want to rescue dogs. They find a dog's abandonment heartbreaking. They want to give it a better life and make up for past wrongs. But just because you feel sorry for a dog does not necessarily mean you will be the right owner for it. You will have to look beyond that beguiling face pressed up against the kennel mesh and consider how well you will be able to fulfil the dog's needs.

Be aware of how much Collies can vary in character. Just because you once owned one who had a superbly easy and undemanding nature, it does not mean they will all be the same. If you see an incredibly attractive, or even pedigree show quality, Border Collie who has been the inmate of a rescue kennel for some time, you have to ask why. Why hasn't anyone else grabbed it, if it is that wonderful a dog?

When we say dogs and people are made for each other, we mean that they have an ability to understand and fulfil each other's needs without conflict. But conversely some people, no matter how well-meaning, are definitely not made for some dogs, and we have to appreciate that and be guided by judgements more experienced than our own.

Would-be Collie owners often state that it is harder to get a dog from a rescue centre than it is from a breeder, without realising that they are summing up half the breed's problem in a nutshell. Dogs acquired too easily frequently become dogs disposed of too easily. Rescue centres are not in the business of recycling dogs, already stressed from past disposal, round endless short-lived 'trial and error' homes, with the dog paying the price for any error. They want committed and permanent homes.

People are not always to blame when dogs need new homes. Sometimes owners die, or are evicted from their homes. There may be many other genuine reasons why dogs can no longer be kept, from a relationship split to a new job abroad. Often people, as well as dogs, can be at the mercy of pressures and circumstances that they could not foresee or control.

Choosing Your Rescue Collie

If a particular Collie has caught your eye in a rescue centre, then here are some helpful questions and observations you should bear in mind:

How much do you know about the dog's background?

Could it have come from a dubious breeder?

Is it the product of pure working stock?

What was its former home like?

Why has the owner got rid of it?

Sometimes a dog's true background will not be known, and the reasons given for the dog's disposal will not always be truthful, which is why a rescue centre offering expert assessment of a dog's basic character and pet potential is so crucial.

Does the dog seem to be suffering from excessive stress, e.g. cowering despondently in the back of its kennel or displaying defensive aggression?

Collies and 'Kennel Stress'

When looking at Collies in rescue centres, please bear in mind that as a breed they can have problems coping with a kennel environment. The confinement, noise, outside activity levels and lack of mental stimulation often combine to make rescue kennels very stressful places for Collies to be, especially long-term.

Problems Collies can have in kennels through stress include weight loss and the development of 'manic' behaviour patterns - e.g. circling, leaping up and down, barking - to release tension, frustration or general unease. Alison Taylor, a behaviourist working at The Dog's Home, Battersea, in London, having studied this Collie phenomenon at length, also believes that a dog's more 'disturbed' behaviour in kennels can often be linked to the strength of its individual 'working instinct'. This in turn can help to establish what sort of future home the dog would be best suited to.

If you see a Collie behaving in a seemingly 'mad' way in kennels, then it could well be a very different dog once taken out of this environment. For this reason, if you like the general look of the dog, it might well be worth asking to see how it behaves when you meet it in an exercise area or office at the rescue centre. And also ask the staff to give you more details about the dog's general personality and behaviour when out of kennels.

Make the most of any behavioural advice you can get from a rescue centre. Most will have consultants in this field to offer guidance. Tell them about the circumstances and experience you can offer the dog you are interested in. Discuss what potential behaviour problems the dog might, or might not have and what sort of remedial training/handling might be required of you if you took the dog on.

Is the dog on any on-going medication? If so, which kind and why? Does it have any known health problems/particular aversions, e.g. to children, other dogs etc.

From all this information you will be building a profile of the sort of dog you might be taking on. You can also expect any good rescue centre to thoroughly grill you about your suitability as the dog's next, and hopefully permanent, new owner.

Early Days

Many new owners of rescue Collies find the first few weeks with them are the worst. However, this could also be a honeymoon period, with problems only arising later. It is important to understand that this is a common occurrence, not an immediate indication of owner/dog failure. As mentioned before, a rescue Collie can typically arrive in a new home with a burden of stress. A new home then means more stress. Stress usually makes Collies do silly and barely tolerable things, ranging from destructiveness - especially when left alone - to over-boisterousness and readier aggression.

When stress reaches a certain level in a Collie (see the previous chapter), it can be sustained for quite some time. When Collies keep going back to rescue centres after only a week or two in a new home, it is because in many cases their stress levels have never had the right circumstances and time scale in which to begin winding down.

Undeniably a stressed Collie can be pretty stressful, but while owners and dogs are continually winding each other up, there will never be a solution to this problem. Someone has to break the cycle, and people are usually in a better position to do this than dogs.

Remember, few people go on acquiring, and rescuing, Collies because they are incorrigible martyrs and masochists. They do it because they know how uniquely rewarding, and very special, these dogs can be when they finally get an owner they can trust and respect, and who cares enough to want to learn their language.

Happy Endings

So far we have looked at the possible problems and pitfalls that can be attached to rescuing Collies. But let us not forget how often there can be happy endings.

Earlier in this book, I mentioned how my own rescue Border Collie, Kim, was the inspiration for all I subsequently hungered to know about this testing, yet ceaselessly fascinating breed. After taking her on when she was 13, lost in an internal torment of psychological despair, and discarded as worthless, there were some very anxious times, some very daunting and challenging times, but never any moment of regret.

Sometimes the journey out of hopelessness with a troubled Collie can be long and hard, but few will not repay you for the effort. Between the ages of 13 and 15 Kim went on to win 26 show titles in veteran and obedience classes. While not bad for a 'worthless' dog, these prizes were nothing, in terms of a reward for persistence, compared to the knowledge of how much faith and confidence she had regained in order to win them. All over the country, and around the world, there are lots of very special people who have turned the lives of traumatised Collies around and, in the process, have probably learned a lot about themselves. Some of their stories make very harrowing reading, but also bear testimony to the force of a Collie's spirit, and the determination of the human soul.

Lizzie Angrave and Poppet

Lizzie Angrave, a former veterinary nurse now working as an estate manager in Buckinghamshire, rescued Poppet in 1996 when he was around five months of age she says:

It is hard to forget the day Poppet was brought into the veterinary surgery where I was working by a dog warden. He was obviously suffering tremendous fear and pain and would not let any of us go near him. He looked clearly terrified. The dog warden said he had been alerted to Poppet by a neighbour of his former owners. She said the dog had been left tied to railings for three days, and his continual howling and screaming sounded like an animal in absolute agony.

It was only when we anaesthetised Poppet that we realised why. The first thing that hit me was the terrible smell of burning flesh; like meat that had been left to overcook on a barbecue. There was also something odd-looking about Poppet's skin under his coat; all wrinkled as if he had mange or a bad flea allergy. But to our horror as we shaved off the coat, the skin began to come off with it. One entire half of his body was still smouldering from appalling burns that we later discovered had been caused by having a whole pan of hot chip fat tipped over him. He had been left tied up with no subsequent treatment, and in continuing agony from these burns, for three days. It could have been longer if the dog warden had not rescued him. It was unbelievably cruel.

Because Poppet was an RSPCA case there were not, I knew, unlimited funds available to treat him. And nobody thought he could survive such injuries. It was also hard to see how he could ever trust another human being again. But as Poppet came round from the anaesthetic, there was just this one poignant moment when he began wagging his tail at me and I was utterly moved. I vowed then that if this dog was going to die then it wasn't going to die here untouched and unloved and totally alone in the prison of a veterinary kennel. In some inexplicable way I knew he had chosen to put his trust in me and I couldn't turn my back on that. I knew if he'd gone to rescue kennels that really would have been the end of him. So I decided to take him home with me, for whatever time he had left.

But even by the next morning, with just a little care and attention, he seemed to be a different dog, so I decided to do all I could to save him. There were months and months of treatment and surgery ahead for him. Sometimes whole saucers full of dead skin had to be taken off him. But he was a real survivor.

During surgery visits, we also discovered that his back leg and hip had sustained multiple fractures, different ones dating back to when he was eight weeks old. These were clearly the result of being kicked repeatedly, and the injuries have left permanent damage, which limit the amount of exercise Poppet can take.

As Poppet got older there were some problems with dominant aggression. He had got used to being the centre of attention. This was mostly cured with behavioural guidance and him having the 'snip'. He also has a tendency to nip when under stress and dog training classes and other noisy, bustling environments can put him under stress, so I have to work on this.

Nobody really knows where Poppet originally came from, but we mostly suspect he was the sort of working stock pup you'll see sold at the roadside for £50. It is likely he had very little early socialisation with other people or dogs, so he's come a pretty long way. I know, because of the injuries he has sustained, he will never live as long as other Collies, which makes him all the more precious. But he has become an amazingly huge part of me. My best friend, my soulmate, my shadow. Wherever I turn, he's there. I now find it impossible to imagine life without him.

Poppet's former owner was successfully prosecuted for cruelty and banned from keeping another animal for life.

Ann Jones & Bobby

Ann Jones, a dance teacher from Carmarthenshire, Wales, originally rescued 'Bobby', a blue merle Collie, in 1994, when he was just over a year old. Here she recounts his story:

Everybody tells me that Bobby's life reads like a film script. No one can believe what he has suffered and survived. His story, as we were to discover, dates back to when he was first abandoned as a puppy in a local dog pound. He was always a very sad puppy, bullied and very withdrawn. No one gave him a home until he was seven months old, then the man who did take him on left him chained to rubble by the side of the road.

That is where we first saw him. He looked so weak and frail we thought he must be about 16 years old. He was also very thin. One day my father went over to give him a tin of cat food and he wolfed it down. I think his fate was sealed with my family from that day. There was something in my father that Bobby recognised as hope for the first time in his life.

Bobby

Bobby's owner eventually went away and left him, so we got him back out of the dog pound. But we were just beginning to make a happier and secure life for him when he was kidnapped while out on a walk. Some instinct rapidly told me that he was in big trouble, and he was. Later we discovered the full horror of what happened to him.

Four men had snatched him from a field and taken him to a disused garage. There they tortured him repeatedly for around seven hours. They fractured his jaw, skull and collar bone with a golf club and throttled him so tightly with rope, plastic bags and a shoelace that he was barely alive. After that they left him for dead, tied to a railway line to get finished off by the next train.

But by some miracle, I was drawn down to the railway line while out looking for him, and found him. Our other dog, a Jack Russell called Sally, actually saved his life by frantically pounding at his chest with her paws and snorting up his nose. They had become devoted to each other, and without her and what she did to keep him going I think he would not have survived.

For eight weeks after this ordeal he hung between life and death as a result of his injuries. Behaviour experts all warned me that, even if he should survive he would be half-crazed with fear and aggression and would never be safe with another human being again. But I just believe that, once we'd found him, he knew he'd have something to live for, and that is why he pulled through. It took a lot of time to nurse him back to health, mentally and physically.

For the first two months after his kidnap he literally squealed in terror any time we went outside the house. It pains me that his attackers could never be prosecuted, through lack of sufficient evidence, but at the same time I feel it is a miracle that his faith in people has not been totally destroyed. He is still very nervous of some men, and in some situations, such as anyone raising a golf club, but he has been helped tremendously by the dedicated time put in on him by a local experienced dog trainer.

He has never stopped being a loving dog towards us, and his temperament remains sweet enough for me to use him as a PAT (Pets As Therapy) dog, visiting the sick and elderly in hospitals and retirement homes. No one ever thought that possible after the suffering he has endured in his life. But we always knew he was a very special dog and that's why we never gave up on him.

Corinna Wallbank & Meg

In 1994 Corinna Wallbank, a cattle herdswoman from Lancashire, rescued Meg, a two year old abandoned Border Collie. She recalls:

One evening I suddenly got an anxious phonecall from a woman who knew of my interest in Collies, asking if I'd help her. She said some youths had been spotted torturing four dogs up at some disused farm buildings near me. When we got there the youths had fled, but the scene we found was appalling and unforgettable. One dog had died as a result of injuries and starvation and another had to be put down later for the same reason. It seems the neglected dogs had all been dumped there by someone else before the youths had found them.

Of the two surviving Collies, there was Meg and another male dog. The male dog escaped the worst harm and was later re-homed. Then there was Meg, who had been shot. Like all the other dogs she'd also had fireworks tied to her tail and set off, and her coat was covered with oil which the youths had then attempted to set alight.

Seeing the state of her,a local vet had wanted to put her down. But I begged her not to. When I had gone to release Meg from the wall she had been tied to, the tip of her tail just slowly began to wag, as if to say at last here was someone who wasn't going to hurt her. And I wanted to give her a chance.

It took four hours to clip out her damaged and oily coat, and it was another two years before it fully grew back again. With care and understanding she finally began to blossom, but the early days with her weren't always easy. There was an occasion when she bit me. We never discovered what the trigger for it was, but one can understand why at the start she was a very fearful dog.

Following this incident we changed her diet to much lower fat and protein levels, and changed a lot of other things about her training and lifestyle, and she has never done it since. I also thought she might need a job of work to do, so I began training her to work with me. At first I was very apprehensive, as anyone would be letting an untested dog round up cattle worth around £1000 each. But she did extremely well and today I never regret for a moment taking her on. Twice she has literally saved my life when I was charged by heifers. I know that if she had to, she'd lay down her life for me. But I would never want to put her in such a position. The adoration and the love that has grown since rescuing her are mutual.

Such is her temperament today that I even use her as a PAT dog. She no longer fears people touching her. If there were a way you could clone another dog exactly like Meg I'd do it tomorrow.

There are many things such powerful tales of suffering and redemption can tell us about people and dogs. It is commonly said that dogs, and particularly Collies, can be highly unpredictable. But sometimes you have to wonder how dogs ever reconcile themselves to a species that asks for trust on the one hand, and on the other can be so treacherously brutal and cruel, when even we can find no answer for it.

Many people also believe that canine rescue is just about people helping dogs. But equally it can be about dogs helping people to be better people. Anyone who has ever experienced fear or helplessness, vulnerability or pain, injustice or insecurity has the ability to understand and communicate with the mind of a rescue dog. Sometimes people discover qualities in themselves they never knew they had until a dog came along and needed them.

Chapter 9

COLLIE HEALTH AND GROOMING

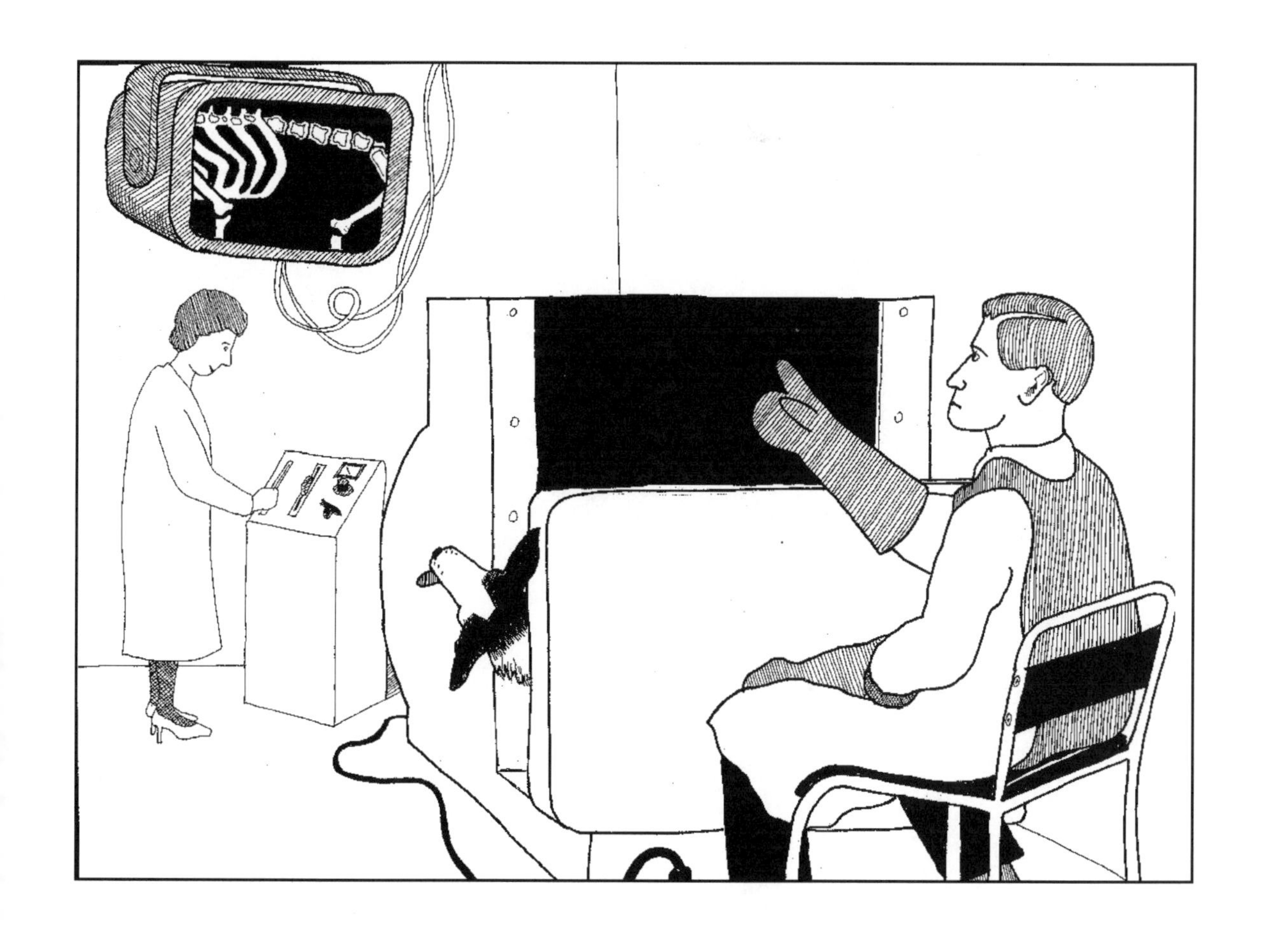

Collies are generally thought to be a pretty healthy breed, as one might expect of dogs who have evolved from tough working stock and a broad and diverse range of sound bloodlines. However, no breed 'stands still' genetically. It constantly evolves according to the demands put upon it to adapt. In domestic dogs this usually means adapting to the demands of humans rather than those more naturally exacted by their environment.

In the last few decades Collies have gained an appeal far beyond their traditional farming roots. History teaches us that whenever any dog breed suddenly attracts a wide appeal and demand, there can be dangers. Certain bloodlines can be 'over-used' either to simply increase the turnover of dogs for the pet market (as happens in "puppy farms") or to keep repeating or 'perfecting' desired or fashionable pedigree looks and characteristics. The end result can mean more dogs within the breed suffering 'hereditary' defects of health, physique or temperament. This is true of any dog breed, not just Collies, and conscientious breeders will always have such risks at the back of their minds.

But just as it can be hard for any Collie owner to know its dog's full past genetic history, do bear in mind how difficult it can be for even the best Collie breeders to always get 'perfect' puppies out of 'perfect' dogs. Sometimes 'faulty' genes will skip several generations before recurring. Sometimes dogs carry genetic imperfections without necessarily suffering from them themselves. Also, if an hereditary disorder has a late onset factor, as with some eye disorders which develop at three years of age or more, it may only be discovered after a dog carrying it has been bred from.

While it might be useful to know what sort of disorders have become particularly associated with Collies in recent years and the treatments available, be aware that 'associated' does not necessarily mean rife within the breed. At least, thankfully, not at present.

Collies are dogs which were originally bred in line with the laws of nature, in the sense that only the fittest and smartest survived. But the more they continue to be bred for other reasons, the less future generations of Collie owners will be able to take this healthy legacy in their dogs for granted. There are many people in this world who care deeply about preserving the overall soundness and intelligence of Collies. Hopefully the future of the breed will lie in what they believe in preserving and what they do to keep it preserved, rather than in any other hands.

Inherited Disorders

The following is a brief rundown on disorders with an hereditary factor in Collies, or which are known to occur in the breed. Your vet will always be the best person to give you more detailed diagnoses, guidance or advice. Also, for more information on eye/joint testing schemes and epilepsy, see advice section at the end of this book.

Collie Eye Anomaly (CEA)

The term 'Collie Eye Anomaly' can be deceptive, because it is far less prevalent in Border Collies than Rough or Smooth Collies. However, as it is still seen in Border Collies, be aware that pups can be tested for it from about six weeks of age.

The disease is hereditary and due to a recessive gene which affects the normal development of the puppy's eye in the womb. The defect, which can only be seen by a veterinary opthalmoscope examining the retina and fundus (back of the eyeball), can affect one or both eyes. Depending on how badly distorted or damaged the retina and other deeper structures of the eye appear to be, the dog could suffer minor visual impairment to total blindness in one or both eyes. It is not painful, but there is no treatment or cure and any dogs suffering it should not be bred from.

Progressive Retinal Atrophy (PRA)

Again affecting the retina, and only recognised in its early stages by the use of an opthalmoscope, PRA comes in two forms; Generalised PRA and Central PRA. And as its 'progressive' name suggests, this condition can develop and increasingly worsen in dogs of any age in adulthood. Unlike CEA, early testing will not always highlight a dog likely to suffer from PRA in the future. Both PRA forms are the result of defects to the retina, or light-sensitive layer of the eye. Generalised PRA is usually first noticed when a dog appears to suffer from a loss of peripheral vision and night blindness. GPRA can degenerate to total blindness. Central PRA (CPRA) is more often seen in Collies than the above. This form of retinal disease is often initially noticed when the dog can see moving objects well but seems unable to pick out static people or objects from their background. The vision is better in dim, rather than bright, light. Although once again there is no treatment for this problem, it does not necessarily result in complete blindness later.

Primary Lens Luxation

This is a potentially very painful condition, leading to blindness, where the ligament (or zonule) holding the lens at the centre of the eye weakens, causing the lens to subsequently slip or displace. Its first clinical signs can usually be seen from three to seven years of age. These include abnormal sensitivity to light, excessive tear production and spasms of the eyelid; all typical responses to ocular pain.

Without prompt surgical intervention to remove the lens of the eye, dogs may be in persistent pain, particularly where the condition has the added danger of leading on to secondary glaucoma, intensifying ocular pressure and the risk of blindness. Sometimes PLL affects both eyes, one in advance of the other.

While it is easy to panic at the thought of a dog suffering from partial or progressive blindness, it does not necessarily mean the end of the road for one who is fit and healthy in all other regards. Many dogs cope better than humans with vision loss, using their noses and other acute senses to pilot their way around familiar surroundings - though unfamiliar ones may require more help from owners.

If you have two dogs, one blind and one not, it can be common for the sighted one to act as the other dog's 'guide'. Naturally, however, a dog with poor or lost vision will require owners to make adjustments, ensuring the dog can never get out from secure environments and into danger. As with deafness (see below) you may have to develop new training commands and methods to maintain successful communication with your dog. Your vet, or nearest training classes, should offer help not just on how to do this, but can also point you to other owners who have successfully dealt with such disabilities in their dogs.

Deafness

Due to a known tendency for some Collie puppies to be born deaf, most good breeders will have whole litters screened for this disability before selling them on, and should be able to provide you with the relevant paperwork to prove that such testing has been done. Congenital deafness in a puppy may require many adapted training methods and use of hand-signal commands, but as with blindness, lots of Collies go on to cope with it very well under the care of sympathetic and well-informed owners.

If you suspect that your puppy may have been born deaf, but cannot be sure, your vet will need to refer you to a hearing specialist to undergo properly conclusive tests. Some Collies may have less hearing loss than others, but due to the adept ability of this breed to read human body language, you will never be truly sure of the extent of it until such tests are made.

Epilepsy

Primary epilepsy is thought to have an hereditary link and usually first fits are seen when a dog is between one and two years of age.

For owners with no previous knowledge of epilepsy in dogs, a first fit can be a very alarming experience, depending on its severity. As with humans, there can be 'petit mal' attacks, localised to just one part of the brain. Less severe, they manifest themselves in a host of symptoms ranging from a noted 'mental absence', leg twitching or a sudden 'personality change' and bouts of uncontrollable barking. 'Grand mal' fits, affecting the whole brain, will be more dramatic and unmistakable. Most often happening when the dog is at rest, symptoms include collapse and often loss of bladder and bowel control. The dog may chomp its jaws and salivate profusely while its lips are drawn back. There may also be an open but unseeing look in the dog's eyes and rigid, paddling movements made with the legs.

Fits can be highly unpredictable in frequency and severity, but owners will need to learn to keep a cool head while such attacks are going on (usually for two to five minutes). Reduce any excess noise (e.g. music, T.V.) and light in the surrounding environment and ensure that the dog cannot damage itself on any nearby hard or sharp objects. Do not try to sit the dog up or pull its tongue out of its mouth. The latter could result in you getting bitten.

Medication today can do much to improve the life quality of epileptic dogs, together with greater knowledge and advice (see advice chapter at the end of the book) on how to manage the condition. Better information and help will also allow owners to see their dog's epilepsy in a less frightening light.

Sometimes primary epilepsy can be confused with other forms of the condition caused by factors like a head injury or brain tumour, or other diseases known to affect the brain, such as malfunction of the liver or kidneys. Veterinary tests should help to rule these out.

Hip Dysplasia (HD) and OCD (Osteochondritis Dissicans)

Both of the above conditions, affecting joint structure and development, were rare, if not unknown, in early lines of working Collies. Although, compared to some other breeds, the incidence of HD and OCD in Collies remains relatively low, both need to be known about.

In simple terms, Hip Dysplasia is a hip joint that is, or has become, malconstructed. In a normal dog, the top of the thigh bone (or femoral head) fits snugly into the corresponding cup-shaped pelvic socket (or acetabulum), allowing comfortable and easy movement over distance, or when the dog has to jump or perform other athletic tasks.

Although varying in degrees of severity among dogs affected, HD is typified by a bad femoral head/acetabulum fit, subsequently making the joint unstable and causing the dog pain after prolonged activity or sudden athletic bouts. X-rays confirming the problem usually show a very shallow hip socket and a distorted femoral head. Early symptoms of HD are generally seen in growing young dogs around the age of five to nine months. There will be noticeable pain or lameness in the dog after exercise, or the dog may seem reluctant to put much weight on its back legs when getting up after sitting for a prolonged period. It will also be reluctant to jump or climb stairs.

HD is a condition where prevention, rather than any later treatment, will do most to help your dog. As mentioned in chapter five, it is now known that bad nutrition (either too rich, or too poor a diet) and over-exercise in growing dogs does much to aggravate both HD and OCD, even if there is also an hereditary factor. Making young dogs stay too long in uncomfortable positions for the hips (e.g. sitting), and allowing them to get too obese will also make matters worse.

Once dogs are known to have HD, their exercise will have to be limited and their weight kept down. Corrective surgery may help some more severely affected dogs, but it is not cheap. Your dog may also need medication to cope with any continuous pain. When diagnosed early and correctly managed, many dogs with HD can live a pretty good life, though they will always have a higher risk of osteoarthritis, as a secondary complication of the condition, when they are older.

To minimise the possibility of HD in your dog, you will need to know whether its parents were ever 'hip-scored' under the British Veterinary Association/Kennel Club hip scheme. Under this scheme, hips are X-rayed and assessed by a BVA expert panel for any sign of abnormality once they are over a year old.

The experts assess nine different features of each hip joint. The minimum score for each hip is 0, which is a perfect hip joint, moving up to a maximum of 53 for a very poor one. A total score for both hips, therefore, ranges from 0 (perfect) to 106 (extremely bad). The breed average for Collies is 13. Obviously if you get a dog from a breeder who can assure you, with the provision of relevant paperwork from tests, that parents of its litters all have low hip scores (i.e. 13 or under) this does look promising - and often is. But sometimes, puppies with perfect joints emerge from parents who have never been hip-tested, and parents with seemingly promising scores can have the odd pup with poor joints. Sadly the only real guarantee about HD or OCD in any dog is that if you do not know how to spot it and manage it early on, it can only get worse.

Osteochondritis Dissicans

This is a disease affecting developing bones and joints (most commonly the shoulder and elbow) in growing dogs from about four to nine months of age. Once again, although it is thought to have an hereditary factor, it can be greatly worsened by wrong diet and excessive exercise during late puppyhood.

In growing dogs, cartilage plates on the joint surfaces of limb bones eventually convert into bone. When a dog has OCD, this cartilage, instead of fully converting to bone, grows thicker and thicker until it cracks when the joint is under stress. Eventually a piece of cartilage can break away from the underlying bone and lie loose within the joint capsule, causing pain and lameness.

A surgical operation to remove such loose cartilage can bring relief, as can specific anti-inflammatory and cartilage-protecting drugs in the early stages. Like HD, it will be made worse by any diet that stimulates rapid growth or is over-loaded with mineral supplements. As in the case of HD, screening of dogs via X-ray for OCD before they are bred from would do much to help limit its incidence in all dogs.

Selective Breeding For Health

Inherited disorders flourish when breeders take insufficient care to eradicate them.

To realise just how effective a 'fault eradication' programme can be in committed hands, look no further than the International Sheep Dog Society's Eye Testing Scheme, in force over the last couple of decades. To be eligible for ISDS registration, puppies must now come from eye-tested parents, and in adulthood, ISDS registered dogs competing at National Sheep Dog Trials (i.e. the top working dogs in the country) must also have their eyes tested annually at these events.

In the 20 years since this scheme has been in operation, the incidence of PRA in tested dogs has come down from 14% to less than 0.25%. It has worked because of the committed efforts of farmers, the British Veterinary Association (who carry out the testing) and the ISDS to keep the precious top working Collie 'sound', and also because the results of eye tests are published by the ISDS, which means dogs who have failed will exclude themselves from a bright breeding future.

Any ISDS registered Collie, or pedigree Collie registered with the Kennel Club is eligible for testing, for all ocular abnormalities, via the BVA/KC/ISDS Eye Scheme. See the Advice section at the end of this book for further details.

All-Round Health

With luck, your Collie will be free of any of the above problems with an hereditary basis. But even so, good health in any dog is not something to take for granted. We need to be continually alert to any developing ailment or illness, not just because we care about our dogs, but because early anticipation can save an animal much future pain, or even its life.

Apart from the most basic procedures for health such as vaccinations and regular worming, here is a top to toe rundown you can routinely give your dog while grooming it. Starting with:

Ears

A Collie's ears should smell earthily sweet and be clean and free of any noticeable soreness, redness, irritation or discharge; any of which could suggest infection or mite infestation, or some foreign body such as a grass seed causing inflammation.

Most ear problems in dogs have obvious early symptoms. The dog will continually shake its head, or scratch at the offending ear, or the ear will be held in a droopy fashion. Cleansing of ears with a proprietary lotion can help prevent dust, dirt and bacteria going too much further, but should not be necessary frequently with healthy ears.

The inner ear should never be subject to prodding and poking by non-expert hands. If ears begin to smell pungent and sour, or an infection seems to have taken root, veterinary help will be required to determine the cause. These range from bacterial, yeast and fungal infections to foreign bodies or an allergic reaction, each requiring appropriate treatment. Your vet can also advise you how to deal with excessive amounts of wax in the ear canal.

Eyes

We have already covered at length serious conditions affecting Collies' eyes with an hereditary factor. But any dog can be prone to conjunctivitis or eye injuries.

In healthy eyes, the inner lining of the eyelids (or conjunctiva) are pink rather than red. Conjunctivitis, whether caused by a scratch or other injury to the cornea, or a bacterial invasion, causes these linings to become swollen and inflamed. There will normally be an accompanying sticky discharge. Often one of the best ways to give quick relief for such a condition is to bathe the affected eye(s) with contact lens fluid or cooled boiled water from a kettle. But many cases require specific veterinary treatment, in the form of eye drops, to make them clear up properly.

Any injury to a dog's eye, e.g. a cat scratch or grass blade scratch to the cornea, can be extremely painful and potentially serious without prompt veterinary attention to limit subsequent infection and corneal damage. Sometimes you will not be able to see a distinct wound to the cornea, which is why vets use a special dye to highlight otherwise invisible damage.

As conjunctivitis and eye injuries can result in similar symptoms, do consult your vet if in any doubt. Also bear in mind that very red or bloodshot eye whites in a dog, with a discharge and accompanied by other symptoms such as listlessness and poor appetite, can be a sign of a high blood toxicity or a major infection in the dog's body. Again, if in doubt, consult your vet.

Apart from known hereditary disorders, most Collies have very healthy eyes. But any sudden changes to them should always be noted and checked out.

Noses

Contrary to popular myth, a cold wet nose in a dog isn't always a reliable indicator of health. Just as some dogs with cold, wet noses can be ill, some with warm dry ones can be perfectly healthy. So you will need more certain evidence to assess health.

Noses that run continually, especially with an excessive watery discharge, moving on to a more purulent and bloodstained form, signifies infection: it can be a result of a foreign body trapped in nasal passages, or rhinitis caused by bacteria, viruses or fungi. Even with veterinary intervention, some forms of rhinitis can be stubbornly persistent. If the foreign body in the dog's nose cannot be easily seen and removed with tweezers - which is not the easiest job in even the most docile of dogs - surgical removal may have to be the answer to the problem.

Also be aware of a condition with an hereditary factor called 'Collie nose'. In dogs rather than very young Collie puppies, which have pink pigment patches on their noses which later change colour, it is typified by itchy, crusty areas made worse by excessive rubbing. Sunlight seems to exacerbate these pink, itchy areas. Sometimes bathing with mild antiseptic helps to clear them up but if not, seek veterinary advice.

Teeth and Gums

Regular efforts to maintain oral hygiene and all-round dental care in your dog, from an early age, will save it much discomfort and pain in later life.

Although Collies tend not to suffer from the sort of dental and gum abnormalities that can plague other breeds, their teeth will need to be kept clean of the plaque and tartar that leads to later problems. Plaque and tartar building up on the teeth, and especially around the gum line, harbour bacteria which not only smell unpleasant but can also cause periodontal (or gum) disease. This means painfully red and sore gums, abscesses and even loosened teeth as infection takes hold deep into dental roots and jawbone.

Once tartar on a dog's teeth has reached a critical cemented-on level, it will be hard for the owner to remove, so a trip to the vet will be required for a professional de-scaling and polishing under anaesthetic. This trauma and expense could have been saved by merely cleaning your dog's teeth a few times a week. You can do this with a soft baby's toothbrush, available from chemists, and a special dog toothpaste from a petshop or your vet, or just diluted bicarbonate of soda in warm water. Do not scrub too hard at the gums, as this can make them inflamed.

The earlier you start this procedure with your dog, the quicker he or she will get used to it as part of a regular grooming routine. Dogs not used to having it done may put up quite a bit of resistance at first, but do persevere, even if at the beginning you can only do one or two teeth at a time. Make a fuss of the dog if it lets you do this, and gradually you will be able to progress on to a wider area as the dog understands you are carrying out an essentially non-threatening, if baffling, regular task.

While cleaning your dog's teeth, check out any other potential problems. Chipped or broken teeth, for example, can be extremely sensitive and painful and can also mean an ensuing abscess as infection enters exposed dental pulp. Swelling under the eye or under the jaw could also indicate an abscess in the root of a tooth. Dogs are said to be able to tolerate pain better than humans, but anyone who has experienced dental agony themselves would understand how unfair it is to leave a dog unrelieved of such distress.

Sometimes owners cannot believe the difference it makes to the character and liveliness of an irritable and depressed dog once they have got a long term canine dental problem sorted out. All the more reason for keeping a regular and alert eye on dental health.

Not all general practice vets have the expertise to perform more complex procedures, like tooth capping, root filling or other operations to preserve teeth that would otherwise have to be removed. If you want more expert advice on your dog's teeth, and your vet cannot refer you to a nearby specialist, see the Advice section at the end of this book.

Sometimes teeth may have fine fractures, or an element of decay, which may not always be readily noticed, but can progress to a painful problem. If your dog is continually pawing or clawing at its nose or mouth, is off its food and more listless than usual, these are indications of tooth trouble that should be further investigated.

Cleaning teeth apart, plenty of chewing material, for example rawhide chews, chew toys and hard biscuits, will also help dental health. If your dog has clean teeth yet still suffers from persistent, rather than temporary bad breath, it might be wise to rule out the possible development of more serious health problems, such as those affecting the kidneys or digestive system.

Body

A Collie with a smooth coat is best rubbed over daily with something like a hound glove (a ribbed rubber glove, available from pet shops) or soft brush to maintain sheen and remove surface debris. These products will not scratch the dog's skin. Your Collie's tail will also need to be gently combed out. Collies with longer top coats, and denser undercoats, can be groomed in the following way:

First, from tail root to head, brush the coat against its normal lying direction fairly vigorously, but not enough to scratch the skin. Then brush the coat back into its normal direction. Finish off with a thorough combing, paying particular attention to any knots behind the ears, in the tail or in the breeching or 'trousers' around the tail.

Normally, a once or twice weekly vigorous brushing, and a daily combing, should keep your Collie looking good, depending on how much debris it regularly traipses home with. Apart from promoting healthy skin by removing clogging matter from the pores, regular combing and brushing keeps up good oil production and spreads it through the hairs - which means a lovely, shiny coat.

Before you begin your grooming routine, run your fingers all over your dog's body, checking for lumps or swellings. Whether benign or not, the sooner you can point these out to your vet, the better the outlook for a cure.

Parasites

Also check for ticks and evidence of fleas. To the uninitiated, ticks can look like greyish warts attached to the surface of the dog's skin - the head and neck being the commonest areas. They will range in size from a small seed to a giant baked bean, or even bigger, depending on how much blood they have consumed. Unless they are around the eyes, give them a squirt of your normal flea product, and they should eventually fall off. For eyes and other delicate areas, smother them in vaseline until they suffocate and drop off. Never pull at a tick to get it off, as the leg and mouth parts of the parasite, embedded in the skin, could be left behind and cause an infection.

Fleas are a number one cause of skin irritation in dogs. Even if you cannot see them, any black specks you comb off the dog onto white paper or cloth, which then turn reddish when dampened, signify flea dirt, and therefore that fleas are present. If your dog is scratching continually, and has already been treated for fleas, it may either have developed an allergic reaction to something in its environment, or be suffering from mange or other mites. These conditions will need veterinary treatment.

Often, Collies become excessively itchy when stressed, giving rise to a heightened sensitivity to allergens. Whether it is the itchiness causing stress, or stress causing the itchiness, is often hard to decide, however, so you will have to tackle both problems together to break the cycle.

Feet

Collie feet are generally very well constructed for endurance. In many dogs, you will notice the thick wads of hair between the pads, which you should keep clean of hardened mud. Do not, however, be tempted to over-prune these wads away. They offer protection against grit, stones and other harmful objects harming the Collie's pads and getting in between the toes.

An active Collie, unless continually run on soft ground, should not have over-long claws, but the the dew claw (the extra claw inside the front leg) will have to be regularly trimmed to avoid it curling inwards, causing pain rather like an in-growing toenail.

Black toenails will always be more difficult to cut than white ones, as the 'quick' cannot be seen, thus it will be easier to nick it and cause bleeding. Some owners prefer vets to cut the dog's toenails or claws. If you do it yourself, you must proceed with caution. Make sure you have sharp clippers designed specifically for animal claws, and only take off minute bits of claw at a time. It is often best to cut small slivers off the claw one week, then repeat the operation the following week once the quicks have retreated a little, rather than to take off bigger chunks in one go. It is also useful to keep a cauterising silver nitrate pencil handy (like nail clippers, they are available from vets). This will help stop any bleeding if you do accidentally cut into the quick. As a rough guide, dog's nails are short enough if you can see that they just clear the ground when the dog is standing. If you are unsure, do ask a vet to give you the best idea of healthy nail length for your dog.

Usually, Collie pads are very tough, but sometimes excessive exercise on rough ground, or hot, dry weather, can cause them to crack a little. Regularly rub a little olive oil or special paw wax into them to keep them supple.

Final Touches

Depending on how fussy you are about your Collie's appearance, you may need to keep breeching and pastern feathers (the hairs growing between hock and heel on back legs) trimmed for tidiness.

Unless your dog repeatedly gets itself in a dirty or smelly state, Collies should not, if regularly groomed, need bathing very often. Sometimes moulting will produce a fair bit of dandruff, which can be helped with a medicated shampoo. (If you would like to try to make your own simple herbal remedies for dandruff, and other grooming lotions, see Collie Health in Chapter 12.) Most Collies that I have known treat baths as one of life's greatest ordeals and insults. Once they have finished climbing up the taps they will not always be that thrilled with you, and might exact revenge with some riotous moisture-shedding stampedes around the house…

Health Emergencies

The following conditions and symptoms all need emergency veterinary attention. Your speed at recognising these symptoms can be life saving:

Gastric Bloat / Torsion

Although more commonly seen in larger and deeper-chested dog breeds, gastric bloat/torsion can also occur in Collies. It is the result of gas from fermenting food, or from air swallowed when eating, building up excessively in the stomach. The pressure from this expansion causes a twisting (or torsion) of the gut, and a restricting impact on circulation that can be fatal. Obviously, the more the gut bloats and/or twists, impeding breathing and circulation and causing harm to other organs, the worse the prognosis for the affected dog.

Signs of bloat to watch out for include a fairly sudden onset of excessive panting and restlessness. Gastric discomfort is making the dog unable to settle, and it may continually retch, or eat grass in an effort to vomit up the cause of its woes. A noticeable, growing tightness or distension of the abdomen means that you should be out of the door as fast as possible, and on your way to the vet.

It would be a great help if someone telephoned the vet ahead of you to warn him or her of the situation, if you cannot do this yourself. This will spare vital minutes of preparation to get your dog anaesthetised, and its stomach pumped free of gas. Should the entrance and exit of the stomach already be closed off through twisting, making such a procedure impossible, more drastic interventionary surgery will be required to release the gas. The dog will also have to be treated for shock.

Sometimes, despite the best efforts of the vet, affected dogs may not be saved. But the key to survival is usually how quickly the dog's owner has spotted the symptoms, and reacted to them. Suggested causes of bloat include: the eating of dried food, followed by copious amounts of water, bolting food and thereby swallowing excessive amounts of air, and exercising too soon before or after a meal.

To prevent attacks of bloat, try switching from dried food to canned food. If persisting with dried food, then limit the amount of water drunk immediately after the meal. Feed the dog alone and put its bowl on a special elevated stand (available from pet shops), to limit its air in-take when feeding. Dogs feeding collectively, rather than singly, often have a far greater competitive tendency to bolt down meals. A small portion of live yoghurt fed to the dog just after the meal may also be beneficial in dispersing stomach gasses. Allow enough time - a good hour - to elapse between exercising and feeding.

Heatstroke

This is a condition that sensible owners should never allow to occur in dogs. Classically, it happens when dogs are left in cars that soon turn into ovens, despite being well-ventilated or initially left in the shade. Because the sun inevitably moves round, and metal intensifies heat, a dog should not be left in a car for longer than 20 minutes on a hot day. However, accidents and oversights do happen in sudden hot weather. If a dog appears to be frantically panting and near to collapse with heat-stroke, you will need to bring its temperature down as quickly as possible. Hose or dowse the dog with cool - but not icy cold - water. Cover the dog with a wet towel or blanket and remove it to a cool area immediately. Add salt to drinking water, at the ratio of one teaspoonful of salt per half-litre.

Even if your dog seems to be recovering, take it to a vet for a checkover, as it could still be suffering from shock.

Road Accident

Every year Collies get run over, either because they have escaped to chase the traffic, or because they have 'bolted' in fright from loud bangs or other frightening stimuli. Equally, many owners have managed to avoid potentially fatal accidents by training them efficiently, since puppyhood, to obey an emergency 'Down!' when necessary. A dog that is trained to obey this command consistently, without hesitation, will have a much safer future.

When dogs get hit by cars, they are not just suffering possible wounds, but also shock. Whether immediate or delayed, shock is a major cause of death in animals after road accidents. Signs of shock after extensive bleeding, trauma or pain are: pale gums, weakness, loss of consciousness, cold skin and rapid, shallow breathing. If your dog has been hit by a car, first keep the dog as warm and quiet as possible, ensuring that its airways are kept clear.

If the dog appears to stop breathing, try mouth-to-nose resuscitation. Cup the muzzle in your hands and gently blow down the nostrils twenty times a minute. Do assess the need for this carefully, as a frightened and shocked dog could easily bite if you get it wrong. A tie or belt gently tied around the muzzle while you perform resuscitation limits this risk, but leaving it on for too long will reduce the dog's ability to get vital air through its mouth.

If you suspect the dog has incurred a spinal injury, get help from someone else to slip it onto a flat board, or other sturdy supportive structure. Otherwise move it, again with help, in a blanket. If the dog looks as if it might attack, you may have to tie a muzzle around its nose while moving it.

Try to ring your vet to explain what has happened, and that you will be on your way with a probable shock victim. The quicker you get to a vet, the quicker life-saving treatment for shock and lost blood can be administered. The first 12 - 24 hours after a road accident can be critical, as the extent of external and internal wounds (particularly haemorrhaging) are assessed, as well as the possible complications of shock.

If the dog is bleeding profusely from an external wound, try tying a pressure bandage, or failing that, a clean cloth or scarf, directly above the wound to stem the blood flow. A clean cloth pushed into the wound and held there tightly, then secured in place with a bandage, will also help.

Instances like these make it clear how wise and essential it is to always carry a prepared First Aid box for dogs (in addition to one for people) handy in the car, or at home. In addition to the sterile bandages, dressings and scissors, animal antiseptic and a roll of gauze tape to construct a makeshift muzzle are simple items that could be vital one day. Likewise, always carry a blanket in the back of the car.

Poisoning

This emergency in dogs is complicated by the wide range of possible toxins that might have been consumed. These show different, or non-specific symptoms, and require different antidotes and treatments.

If you suspect that your dog has been poisoned by something specific, for example slug pellets, rat bait or a toxic plant, let your vet know, as this information will greatly help the vet determine a suitable treatment. One of the most rapid ways of dealing with a dog that you suspect has eaten something poisonous is to make it sick with a teaspoonful of salt, or washing soda, at the back of the tongue. Then give the dog plenty of water. An exception to this treatment would be the possible intake of something caustic or corrosive, such as bleach or battery acid. Such substances could further damage the oesophagus and throat if it were brought back up.

Symptoms of poisoning in dogs range from salivation, excitability, weakness and lack of co-ordination to vomiting, diarrhoea, convulsions and collapse. In all cases, emergency treatment should be sought from your vet.

Pyometra

Usually seen in unspayed and older bitches that have not had pups, and occurring after a heat, Pyometra is a potentially life-threatening womb infection, which builds up with a progressively toxic effect.

Early signs of it in bitches include excessive thirst, loss of appetite, general dullness and bloodshot eyes that exude a purulent discharge as the toxin filters into the bloodstream. Cases of 'open' Pyometra, where pus drains out through the bitch's vulva, are more easily recognised than 'closed' kinds without such an obvious symptom. Both mean prompt veterinary attention to prevent death from blood poisoning, dehydration and shock.

The most effective and permanent solution to the problem is an ovarohysterectomy (i.e. removal of the uterus and ovaries), plus fluid therapy and antibiotic treatment. Many bitches recover extremely well from such an operation, and seem, if anything, to thrive even better when less troubled by hormones. Pyometra is yet another reason why spaying is a sensible option in younger bitches that have no essential need to have a breeding future.

Other Danger Signs

In Chapter 11 we will be looking in particular at the health problems of ageing Collies, so we will not go into that category here. But to conclude this section we will look at symptoms in dogs that are warning signs of trouble to come, and that should be investigated. These include:

Sudden loss of appetite; weight loss or gain; excessive thirst; persistent diarrhoea with or without vomiting; continual coughing and/or exercise intolerance; dullness and lethargy (most abnormal Collie traits!); heavy or abnormal breathing; purulent or bloody discharges from any orifice.

The point of this chapter is not to scare Collie owners into a state of perpetual trepidation about the potential 'health minefield' that lies ahead, because Collies remain one of the toughest and most robust breeds of dogs. But maybe one day something you have read here will help you and your dog, and then you will be glad of what you now know.

Chapter 10

THE COMPETITIVE COLLIE

Collies are born with an urge and need to have something to think about and something to do; some outlet for all their natural mental and physical energies. For this reason, it is perhaps no co-incidence that the popularity of relatively newer canine competitive events, such as Obedience, Agility and Flyball, has risen in line with the trend for owning Collies as pets.

Such events, and Collies, seem to be made for each other. In this chapter we are going to look at all the different kinds of activity open to pet Collies, from pedigree and fun shows to the more seriously testing Working Trials. But do remember that however clever Collies are, no Collie is born knowing what to do in a competition ring any more than it would know how to work livestock without proper training. Just as it can take years of painstaking training to turn a Collie into a top working sheepdog, top competition dogs require similar application and effort from their owners.

Showing

Fond owners always imagine that their Collies possess outstanding looks, but be aware that successfully showing your dog is a little more complicated than it might look at Crufts. First to consider is whether your dog is a pedigree Border Collie, and if so, is it registered with the Kennel Club? These are the two prerequisites for entering showing at top level. However, a pedigree that is not KC-registered can compete in pedigree classes at special Exemption shows, which we will discuss more fully later.

Should your Collie be a pedigree and KC-registered, how well does it conform to the precise 'Breed Standard' laid down for Border Collies - as well as all other pedigree breeds - by the Kennel Club? How well, or not, it conforms to this standard in terms of height, colouring, conformation, and many other characteristics, will determine whether or not you should persevere with its showing career.

Local Ringcraft Clubs and Breed Clubs should have details of the required breed standard for Border Collies and advise you on how closely or not your dog conforms to it. They should also be the first port of call for anyone interested in a showing career with their Border Collie, as they can offer expert advice on how to best exhibit your dog in the ring. (To discover the nearest Ringcraft/Breed club to you, see the Advice section at the end of this book.)

KC-registered Border Collies can enter quite a variety of shows, including single breed shows (i.e. those just devoted to Border Collies and usually run by a breed club) or mixed breed shows (run by general canine societies). Single breed shows are a great opportunity to see many Collie experts in one place. You can pick up a wealth of specialist tips about grooming, presentation, the current most successful exhibitors, and breed lines, etc.

Large numbers of people will compete with their dogs at Open Shows around the country, where any KC-registered dog can enter a class suitable for it. But the most prestigious ones remain the Championship Shows. It is only here that the much sought-after Kennel Club Challenge Certificates (or 'CCs or 'tickets') are up for grabs. Only a limited number of these are available to the very best dogs every year. A dog who wins three CCs is entitled to be known as a Champion.

However glamorous showing might appear to the uninitiated, in reality it entails a tremendous amount of time and hard work. There will be many hours spent travelling, preparing your dog, and hanging around waiting for your classes to start. Unless you are extremely fortunate, it is also unlikely that you will win anything major in the early days, until you have learned a lot more about breeding, exhibiting and the preferences of different judges. Usually, those who secure the most undeniably thrilling top awards will only have done so through dedicated perseverance.

Even if you do have the most stunning-looking pedigree Border Collie - or imagine that you have - do be aware that not all Collies will have a temperament suited to the showring. Long hours of travelling, enforced inactivity, being prodded and manipulated by strangers and being tightly hemmed in with other canines can be quite stressful for many dogs. Therefore temperament in a Show Collie will have to be just as special as everything else.

Exemption Shows

Exemption Dog Shows are so called because they are exempt from many of the

Kennel Club rules and restrictions for shows, and are often events where people get their first taste for showing. Principally, they are informal and fun-orientated shows, usually organised in aid of charity, although the pedigree classes within them can be taken quite seriously, and can also draw some very good dogs. Unlike other dog shows, most entries for them tend to be taken on the day that they run.

Exemption shows are divided into 'Pedigree' and 'Novelty' classes. Typically, Pedigree classes will comprise the following: Any Variety (AV) Puppy (i.e. any pedigree breed, normally aged six months to twelve months, although this will vary according to breed); AV Sporting (breeds); AV Non-Sporting and AV Open (i.e. open to all pedigree breeds). Both KC-Registered and non-KC-Registered pedigree Border Collies can compete in all but AV Sporting. The Best In Show is usually chosen from winners of these pedigree classes. 'Novelty' classes are those where your dog - unless particularly specified - does not have to be a pedigree at all to enter. You can choose to take part, among these, in anything from 'Best Veteran' or 'Best Crossbreed' to 'Best Rescue', 'Prettiest Bitch/Most Handsome Dog' or even 'Dog with the Waggiest Tail.'

Apart from being an overall fun day out, in aid of a good cause, Exemption Shows give many owners the chance to understand and develop better ringcraft and exhibiting techniques with their dogs. Both you and your dog can also make lots of new friends. Increasingly today, these shows are also running some obedience classes, particularly for novices. These provide you with a good opportunity to get started in this discipline too, in an informal atmosphere.

Before we examine Obedience, Agility, Flyball and Working Trials, you should be aware that in order to compete more widely in these disciplines (very informal events excepted), your dog may first have to be put on the Kennel Club's Working Trial and Obedience Register (as dogs who are already KC-registered as pedigrees usually don't have to be). More details of this are in the Advice section.

Obedience

For most competitors, the thrill of Obedience is the way that it can both improve and exemplify the level of communication and control that you have with your dog. But just because you can get your Collie to sit, stay and come back when you want it to - most usually when there are few other distractions - this does not necessarily mean that you are ready for a craft that demands perfection of performance in all tasks. Most people get started in Obedience through their local training club. Indeed, Obedience competitions are mainly organised by such clubs, if not part of a larger general dog show. Starting this way is important, because it gives you a better idea of the sort of precision that will be required - no 'crooked sits', for example, or imperfect positioning at 'heel' - and the training needed to compete successfully in this discipline.

Although some Collies will always be naturally better at Obedience than others, no-one ever gets very far in this sport without hours of diligent practice, and possibly several moments of jumping up and down with frustration in front of a highly bemused dog... Most competitors will start off in a Pre-Beginners class at Open (or Limited) Obedience Shows. There will be five exercises, and a total of 75 points available. Marks are lost for any faults or mistakes. The exercises are:

Heel on Lead

It might sound simple, but the dog must be on your left side, the lead must be slack at all times, and the dog's shoulder should be approximately level and fairly close to your leg while you are walking. The same applies when the judge asks you to move 90 degrees to your left or right, or circle in an about turn. When the judge asks you to 'Halt', the dog must sit straight at your side.

Heel Free

As before, only this time without the advantage - even if this is only psychological - of the lead.

Recall

Whether you choose to put your dog in a down or sitting position, the dog must stay where it is, and in that position, until you call it. The judge will ask you to walk a set distance away from it first, with your back to it. When called, your dog should come straight to you, sit straight in front of you and then go to heel as soon as the judge so instructs.

Extra commands and/or encouragement will be allowed for these above exercises, but not for the following:

Sit/Stay

You and your dog will be directed to a set point in the ring, and you will be told to give a 'last command' to your dog to make it sit there and stay, for a full minute.

Should it have moved during this time, or before you have returned to it and instructed it to move, you will lose points.

Down/Stay

As before, except that the dog will be left lying down and must stay still this time for two minutes. You cannot carry any food or treats into the ring for these exercises, but do praise your dog fulsomely each time he or she completes them well.

From Pre-Beginners, exercises can get more complicated and exacting as you move on to Beginners classes, then Novice, Class A, Class B, Open and - at really top level - Championship Class C. Retrieve tasks, scent discrimination, distance control (the dog must obey sit/stand/down commands from you while you are some distance away) and far more complicated heelwork, at different speeds, will be demanded of your dog as you both progress.

Even if you never get to top level in Obedience, it will do much to improve your overall control and bond with your dog. Hours spent trying to build up better communication with a Collie, and using its mental energy in a constructive way, are seldom wasted.

Agility

To the novice onlooker, Agility contests can look particularly thrilling, with Collies excitedly hurtling around challenging obstacle courses at record speed. But Agility tests are just that: events that demand a high level of both physical fitness and mental alacrity - and that means owners, as well as dogs!

Due to the physical effort involved in these contests, dogs have to be over 18 months old in order to compete. Before that age, their skeletons may not be quite fully formed, and strains or injuries could easily result. They should also be very fit, and will need a fair amount of prior training over obstacles before they can take part.

There are a growing number of Agility clubs around the country, which local dog training and breed clubs should be able to inform you about. They usually keep their own set of the obstacles that you will commonly find in Agility contests. These include:

Hurdles

Rather like equine show-jumps, these are a maximum of 2ft 6 ins high and 4 ft wide, with displaceable top bars to minimise injuries. Sometimes two hurdles of different heights will be put together to form a 'rising spread' jump.

Hoop

Suspended from a frame at a fixed height. Alternatively, a tyre may be used.

Table

A minimum of three feet square. Your dog must lie down and stay on this for a time set by the judges.

Long-Jump

A series of low hurdles, maximum length five feet, which your dog must clear in one leap.

Collapsible Tunnel

Up to ten feet long, this is a cloth tunnel with a rigid, round entrance. Your dog must work its way through.

Weaving Poles

A series of five to twelve poles set a least 1ft 6ins apart, that your dog has to 'thread' or 'weave' its way through.

'A' Frame'

Two upright ramps, placed in an 'A'-shaped angle which your dog must negotiate its way up and down, ensuring that its feet touch special ' contact points' at the base of each ramp.

See-Saw

A pivoted plank, as 'see-saw' suggests, with a maximum length of twelve feet. Your dog must negotiate its way up and down the length of the plank, again while not missing set 'contact points'.

Wishing Well

A Hurdle with a roof to it. It might also be called a 'Lych Gate.'

Most people begin in Elementary Agility classes at shows. They can then work their way up through Starters, Novice, Intermediate, Seniors, Advanced, and Open. But do be aware that the competition gets progressively tougher as you move on. Sometimes over a hundred dogs can be vying for places at bigger shows, and such places can be won or lost by the smallest of time margins, even if you get a 'clear round.'

This sport does demand the highest control of your dog, and exceptionally good communication between you both, at high speed. But if you and your dog have trained well enough, and are truely fit enough for what is demanded, it can also be enormous fun. It is a measure of how naturally good Collies can be at Agility that we are now seeing distinct 'ABC' classes advertised. These are open to, unsurprisingly - 'Anything But a Collie'!

Flyball

Flyball involves several teams of dogs and handlers running against each other - and the clock - in relay. Each dog on a team has to run to a 'flyball box', clearing a series of low hurdles on the way. Once at the box, the dog pushes a pedal to release a ball into the air. It must catch this, and race back to the finishing line the way it came, over the same hurdles. The next dog in its team will then directly follow it, until the whole dog team has completed this task in the fastest time possible.

Most people move on to Flyball from Agility, and again, a local training club is the first place to make enquiries about taking part. Your dog will need to be fit, and properly trained, before entering the competition. Flyball events are far less widespread than Agility at present, but they are gaining in popularity. There are those who think that Flyball can particularly over-excite Collies. But then again, a competitive event that doesn't excite Collies seems near-impossible to invent.

Working Trials

Working trials take place in open country, and can be completed over one day, or over several days, depending what level of achievement you are aiming for in this discipline. Your local training club or specialist Working Trials Society can tell you more about what is involved, and can also discuss with you the sort of training needed to take part in different 'Stakes' - or levels of competition. (See the Advice section in Chapter 12 for more details).

These Trials are about the toughest test of the owner/dog working relationship that you can enter with a pet. Indeed, many of them feature some very professional dog handlers. The five 'Stakes' are, in order of progressive complexity:

1. Companion Dog (CD)
2. Utility Dog (UD)
3. Working Dog (WD)
4. Tracking Dog (TD)
5. Patrol Dog (PD)

Each Stake comprises exercises in Control, Agility and Nosework, with points awarded for each one completed. The complexity of the exercises in each section will vary according to the Stake involved, but will typically break down as follows:

Control

You will need to perform heelwork on and off the lead, with varying speeds and turns, and also moving around people and other obstacles. Good recall will also be required, plus 'Send away and Directional Control' - testing how well you can send your dog to a set distance and get it to obey commands accurately from there. Lengthy Sit and Down Stays will also be required, plus retrieval of a dumb-bell, and steadiness to gunshot - a real test for many more 'nervy' Collies.

Agility

Your dog may have to jump a three feet hurdle (it is normally geared to the size of the dog), a series of jumps, and negotiate a vertical wall of wooden planks.

Nosework

Within a defined area, your dog must search the ground and retrieve a number of articles placed there before the exercise. Points are awarded not just for the articles retrieved, but also for how much control and style the dog can demonstrate in completing the exercise. Your dog will also be required to track, via scent, the route taken by someone unknown to it. This route will be about half a mile long, with many twists and turns. Articles will have been placed along it which the dog must locate.

In many ways, such competitive events are ideal outlets for Collies, giving them the chance to stretch their mental as well as physical energies, and proving that they do possess some quite exceptional skills when they are given an opportunity to shine.

Now that you have a far better idea of all the different sorts of competitive events open to your Collie, and which will keep you - and your pet - happily challenged and occupied, all that remains to be said is: Good Luck!

Chapter 11

THE AGEING COLLIE

Considering the pace at which they live life, many Collies can reach a fairly advanced old age for dogs - over 15 years is not uncommon - and remain pretty sprightly with it. Sometimes this is just down to excellent genes, but the caring and considerate ownership of an ageing dog, plus keeping a keen eye on its health and welfare, can also play a big part in the quality and length of its later life.

Let us now look at the changes that might be occurring in Collies as they get older, and how we might best approach and deal with them.

Exercise

Many Collies continue to whizz around agility rings at the age of 12, but there is still bound to come a day when a normal exercise quota becomes too much for an ageing dog. Collies will always give 100 percent of their effort and try harder than many other breeds to persevere through discomfort, so we must be extra aware of when they might be overdoing it. If a dog repeatedly becomes lame or excessively stiff after its usual walk or exercise, then this level of activity has now become too much for it.

Most older dogs benefit far more from two or three short walks a day, rather than one really long one. This keeps the joints regularly warmed up and loosened, without putting them under prolonged pressure, or further aggravating conditions like arthritis. It also keeps circulation, lungs, heart and the digestive system ticking over more efficiently. But any dog developing severe exercise intolerance suggestive of respiratory or heart malfunction, such as laboured breathing, wheezing and a blueish or purplish tinge to the tongue or gums, will require urgent veterinary attention.

In older dogs, intense 'chasing and jumping' exercise should also be severely limited or curtailed. In a rush of adrenalin and excitement, a dog whose joints are no longer quite so springy or supple could do itself injuries more readily. Such injuries could either worsen existing joint or skeletal problems, or take far longer to recover from. Back legs may also get progressively weaker in older dogs, requiring you to give them extra help in getting over walls or into the car.

Although the use of veterinary-prescribed pain-killers and anti-inflammatory drugs can do much to relieve joint or skeletal discomfort, they must be used wisely. Anti-inflammatory drugs, in particular, if used in an uncontrolled and prolonged manner, can lead to other health problems. Always discuss the pros and cons of this treatment, like that of pain-killers, with your vet.

For details on more natural remedies for a wide range of canine health problems, see the Advice section following this chapter.

Sight and Hearing

Inherited conditions apart (see Collie Health, chapter 9), sight and hearing in older dogs are destined to lose their earlier acuteness. It is important to be observant of these changes, and to appreciate that a dog with less sharp sight and hearing can get lost and disorientated more easily when out with you - especially somewhere less familiar. It will not always hear your call or see where you are, particularly if you are standing still. Sometimes a whistle or a clap of your hands will be more audible than your voice to dogs with failing hearing.

It may be easy to get impatient with an older dog, imagining that it is endlessly dawdling and sniffing things. In reality, it can no longer sustain its rapid pace of old and has to rely increasingly on its nose to evaluate and explore its surrounding environment. Be a bit more understanding, and let bouts of happy dawdling be one of the few privileges of old age in a dog.

Mental Outlook

As a dog ages, it's world view changes. It has a growing sense of vulnerability, due to dwindling faculties, joint or other niggling discomforts, or a general feeling of threatened status. It may become more defensive or 'grumpy'. It may need far more reassurance about its overall security. It may become more 'clingy' with owners.

Even if a Collie's physical powers appear to be waning, never forget how much mental stimulation still matters, and keeps up the dog's morale. There is nothing sadder than a Collie who has been left at home all day to mentally 'rot', just because it can no longer accompany its owner, or other dogs, on longer walks.

If your Collie cannot walk far, why not take it out with you regularly on car journeys or errands, or give it short outings to new and stimulating environments full of novel smells and sights. It still needs to feel 'involved' in pack life. It cannot spend its time at home all day writing books, drawing pictures or making models out of matchsticks. Regular 'nose work' exercises - e.g. finding food hidden in the garden, or scent items while out walking - can also help this process. Older dogs will also want to sleep more, and will not take kindly to being suddenly disturbed or woken up. Bear this in mind, and let them have their peace when they want it.

Feeding and Weight

Obesity can be a major problem in older dogs - and increasingly today, in younger ones, too. Its overall impact on health can mean a much shorter life expectancy. Owners who state that their dogs eat 'virtually nothing' tend to forget the cumulative effect of all those extra little treats, leftovers and scraps from the table. A dog who genuinely eats poorly but still carries much weight should be checked for a condition called Hypothyroidism. This is a glandular malfunction of the thyroid which seriously affects the body's metabolism. It can be treated and stabilised by your vet.

Whether a Collie gets fatter or thinner with age depends on a variety of factors. Usually a dog gets fatter because it is eating more calories than it is expending in exercise. Very soon, it is caught up in a vicious circle, eating as much as before but becoming increasingly unwilling to take much exercise because obesity makes exertion an excessive strain on joints, heart and lungs.

Most obesity, however, will respond to a far more controlled and lower fat diet. There are now many proprietory brands of food for older or overweight dogs, including 'prescription' ones available from your vet. In line with a more restricted diet, exercise needs to be built up gradually.

More often than not, however, dog obesity is more of a problem of human will-power, and limited owner appreciation of the risks their pet is running. But when a dog gets progressively painful arthritis or diabetes as a result of its weight, or dies prematurely of heart failure, it is too late to wish you had acted earlier on the vet's advice. Such dangers apart, an overweight dog will always have a much poorer life quality than a leaner one, in all respects.

When older dogs get leaner, it is often because their digestive tracts are no longer as efficient at absorbing nutrients. But other underlying problems such as cancer, kidney failure and diabetes, need to be ruled out if the weight loss is sudden and dramatic. Much of a leaner look can also be attributed to general muscle loss as the dog gets older.

Many older Collies become 'picky' eaters, unless suffering from an excessive appetite typical of a dog unable to metabolise efficiently what it eats. In old age, quality, not quantity of food, becomes more important. Many dogs seem to thrive on 'home cooking' rather than on commercially prepared diets. Boiled rice or pasta, steamed vegetables (carrots, broccoli, green beans), and a portion of easily digested cooked meat such as chicken or lamb, the occasional egg or bit of offal, seems to suit many older dogs. A teaspoon of bran regularly, and a portion of oily fish (tuna, mackerel or pilchards, but first wash off any excess brine or sauce) can also boost its general condition, as might regular essential fatty acid supplements or cod liver oil.

Before undertaking such a change in dietary regime, do first consult your vet as to how it might suit an individual dog. Ingredients and proportions need to be tailored to a dog's weight, metabolism, and general health.

Remember too, how important it is to maintain a dog's dental health well into old age, with regular cleaning, and chew items and check-ups on any suspect teeth. If a dog can't eat or chew well, it will either not eat enough, or won't chew its food well enough for proper absorption.

Other General Adaptations

Over and above primary concerns about exercise, faculties and diet in older dogs, here are some other considerations to bear in mind:

They will need deep, warm, soft bedding that is always dry, and kept in a draught-free place.

They may need to go to the toilet more often.

They may need their claws clipping more regularly, due to reduced exercise.

Their body thermostats will become less efficient, making them more vulnerable to the effects of excessive heat or cold.

They may need more regular veterinary check-ups - perhaps every three to six months, depending on general health.

Their reactions and limb functions will slow down, taking them much longer to sit or lie down at your command.

They will need to feel that they are still a great part of your life, and be treated with more sensitivity, understanding and kindness.

More Serious Health Concerns of Old Age

Older dogs, like older people, will be more prone to a wide range of health problems resulting from a gradual deterioration of body organs and systems. Luckily, more can be done now to stabilize such problems than ever before.

By the time they have accompanied their pets into old age, most people have grown to know their dogs pretty well. They know when something is suddenly 'not right' about their demeanour, appetite and breathing, thirst, bowel or bladder functions. All such changes need to be reported to your vet to secure the earliest possible remedial treatment.

Keep an eye out also for any developing tumours that are visible. Most common among these will be those affecting the skin, mouth, testes (in older male dogs) and the mammary glands of bitches that have not been spayed when very young. Some may be benign, but your vet can best make that assessment, and this needs to be done as soon as any new 'bump' appears. However worried you may feel about a 'sinister' diagnosis, remember not only that cancer treatment for dogs is improving all the time, but that time spent stalling and worrying is wasted time as far as your pet's recovery is concerned.

For reasons that are not always fully understood, older dogs can also be more prone to what we might perceive as 'strokes', though vets term it Vestibular Syndrome. Pressure building up in the dog's inner ear - whether due to an infection or a circulatory disorder - can cause the dog to lose balance. It may stumble, stagger and move in tight circles, or even collapse. There will also be a pronounced tilt of the head to one side, and rapid eyeball movements known as nystagmus. The onset of such an episode can be gradual, or quite sudden. Although highly alarming for owners, many dogs can recover fairly quickly from this condition if given prompt veterinary treatment, though a degree of head tilt may remain.

It is important to keep the dog quiet and on one level of your house while it is suffering from this condition, so that it cannot fall downstairs or otherwise harm itself while its balance is impaired. Due to the disruption within the inner ear, the dog may also be nauseous and unable to hold down food and water, until the condition begins to improve. A prolonged inability to hold down water will require additional veterinary treatment to avoid dehydration.

Once a dog has had one Vestibular Syndrome episode, there is a risk that it might suffer another one, equally or even more severe. But their occurrence can be highly unpredictable. Some dogs have one or two attacks within a short period, and then never have another within their lifetime. Others will be less lucky.

The Hardest Days

Sadly, not every ailment or incapacity of old age can be overcome indefinitely by veterinary science, and the time may come when we have to consider ending an elderly dog's suffering through euthanasia. When weighing up the right time for this, it is important to put the dog's needs first, over and above our own dread of coping with the dog's loss. No dog suffering constant pain, disability and discomfort has much joy left in life.

Such decisions can involve much courage and heartache. It is to be expected that the days immediately before and after a beloved Collie's departure will seem among the hardest in one's life. But try your very best to be there, preferably in the comforting and familiar surroundings of your home, when your dog is euthanased. It is the only adequate way to repay the lifelong loyalty of an old friend, and to prove to the last that it was never wrong to place its total trust in you.

It is a sad reality that dogs seldom live long enough for most humans. They are destined to only ever share stages of our lives, and not the whole journey. But those parts of the journey that you have shared with a Collie are not likely to ever be forgotten. Whether you are being driven barmy by their energy, awed by their loyalty and willingness, staggered by their intelligence, or raging in fury as they disappear over the hills, life with them is always destined to be eventful. But not for one moment will it ever be dull.

Ultimately, the best, and most rewarding Collies, tend to belong to people who appreciate all their downs as well as ups, and love and value them no less for it. If you have discovered that the Collie is a unique and very special dog, you might put that down to some exceptional genes. Or it might just be that you cared enough, and tried hard enough, to make it that way.

Chapter 12

FURTHER ADVICE

Nobody really knows what the future holds for Border Collies as a breed, or whether in the years ahead the Border Collie will be more commonly owned as a pet rather than as a working sheepdog.

If the Collie is to be most commonly owned as a pet there may be a temptation to alter its current traditional role to better suit human convenience. If dogs are consistently bred to be pets they will display different patterns of behaviour from those of working sheepdogs. There is, however, a danger in such selective breeding. If the working instincts and energies that make the Collie challenging as a pet are bred out, we may also lose the factors that make the breed so intelligent and exceptional. We may lose part of our national rural heritage.

Dogs can never live up to all that we want them to be, as long as we keep changing what we want from them. And sometimes, with Collies, we have to know when they have reached the limits of how they can change to suit us, at which point we might have to change to live more successfully with them.

Many of us can live with great pet Collies, but I suspect that few of us ever live with perfect ones. Most of us seem to tread a fine line between what we learn to tolerate and what we strive to improve. If you find yourself needing more experienced help and advice for your pet, never regard it as an indication of failure. It is, instead, an indication that you care enough about your dog to sense that you could have a better life together. And very often, you can.

Breeders

The following advice sources can help you locate good Collie breeders in your area - whether you are interested in a pedigree dog with show potential, or want one from a line specialising in Obedience, Agility, etc. The International Sheep Dog Society listed below is a particularly valuable source of information on working dogs, working bloodlines and their track records in terms of proven health (e.g. eye screening) and performance.

Do not be surprised, or offended, if many of these advice sources give you a good preparatory grilling about your suitability or commitment levels as a future Collie owner. It is only right and responsible of them to want to ensure that their cherished breed, which has had such problems in the past with inappropriate ownership, only goes to the most fitting homes. Also see the **Finding a Breeder** section in Chapter 3.

THE KENNEL CLUB
1-5 Clarges St
London W1Y 8AB
tel: 0870 6066750

THE INTERNATIONAL SHEEP DOG SOCIETY
47 Bromham Rd
Bedford MK40 2AA
tel: 01234 352672

SOUTHERN BORDER COLLIE CLUB
Mrs S.M. Whittington
13 Cobbs Close
Wateringbury, Maidstone
Kent ME18 5NJ
tel: 01622 813529

EAST ANGLIA BORDER COLLIE CLUB
Mrs K. Kinton
Valley View
Watling St. West, Fosters Booth, Pattishall
Northants NN12 8LD
tel: 01327 830308

MIDLANDS BORDER COLLIE CLUB
Mrs B. Swann
40 Nunts Lane, Coventry
W. Midlands CV6 4HR
tel: 01203 644032

NORTH WEST BORDER COLLIE CLUB
Mrs C. Richardson
Bank House Farm
Mort Lane, Tyldesley
Greater Manchester M24 8PF
tel: 0161 703 8395

BORDER COLLIE CLUB OF GREAT BRITAIN

Mrs J. Cresswell
15 St. Ives Close,
Weeping Cross
Stafford ST17 0HD
tel: 01785 664619

BORDER COLLIE CLUB OF G.B.
(Southern branch)
Mrs A.M. Bridgeman
Foxhill Cottage
211 Lyndhurst Rd
Ashurst
Southampton SO40 7AA
tel: 01703 293258

SCOTTISH BORDER COLLIE CLUB
Mrs J. Hastie
Fliskmillan Cottage
Newburgh, Cupar
Fife KY14 6HN
tel: 01337 870264

WEST OF ENGLAND BORDER COLLIE CLUB
Ms. P. Griffiths
Rystwood
Seven Ash
Bishops Lydeard
Somerset TA44 3AX
tel: 01823 432455

BORDER COLLIE CLUB OF WALES
Mrs S. Jones
Ty Llyn
Braichmelyn
Bethseda, Bangor
Gwynedd LL57 3LR
tel: 01248 602955

BORDER COLLIE BREED COUNCIL
Mrs M. Turner
67 Chaffes Lane
Upchurch
Sittingbourne
Kent ME9 7BH
tel: 01634 366398

Training and Behavioural Advice

Many of the above might help you with useful contacts, if not personal advice, in this area. You can also try:

Association of Pet Behaviour Counsellors, P.O. Box 46, Worcester WR8 9YS tel: 01386 751151 (Your vet will normally refer you to a member of the above.)

The Association of Pet Dog Trainers, Peacocks Farm, North Chapel, Petworth, W. Sussex GU28 9JB

For further advice on **'Calming Signals'** (See Chapter 7: *Collie Stress*) and details of international seminars featuring them, contact: Turid Rugaas, Hagan Hundeskole, Boks 109, 3360 Geithus, Norway.

The **National Canine Defence League** provides fact sheets for a wide variety of behavioural problems. Address details are under Collie Rescue.

A supplementary owner's advice guide to specific Collie behaviourl problems, *'Living with a Border Collie'* is also available from Broadcast Books (0117 9732010) at £4.00 incl. p&p.

Please note: These recommended sources apart, it is vital that anyone you approach - or who approaches you - to deal with any specific 'behavioural' or 'training' problem with your Collie has genuine and lengthy experience of the breed, and does not practice any remedies based on physical punishment or other forms of abuse that could be highly damaging to your dog psychologically. If you have any doubts at all about a training or behavioural advisor, or if they have no proven past credentials, go elsewhere or stick to reputable established sources such as the above.

Collie Rescue

Collies are often available for re-homing through centres run by our main national animal charities. These include the following, who can provide details of your nearest rescue and re-homing centre:

The National Canine Defence League
17 Wakley St. London EC1V 7LT tel: 0207 837 0006

The Blue Cross
Shilton Rd. Burford, Oxford OX18 4PF tel: 01993 822651

The RSPCA
Causeway, Horsham, W. Sussex RH12 1HG tel: 01403 264181

Scottish Society for the Prevention of Cruelty to Animals
Braehead Mains, 603 Queensferry Rd, Edinburgh EH4 6EA tel: 0131 339 0222
Operating on a large and well-established scale there is also:

The Border Collie Trust of Great Britain
Heath Way, Narrow Lane, Colton nr. Rugeley, Staffs WS15 3LY tel: 01889 577058

These apart, there are also many smaller specialist 'Border Collie and Sheepdog Rescue' organisations and agencies, such as the one run by Julie and Gary Nelder in Lincolnshire (01507 313285) mentioned in Chapter 8.

Collie Health

Should you be wanting advice on how to find a canine dental specialist, or further information about testing procedures for eye or joint abnormalities in Collies, contact:

The British Veterinary Association (Canine Health Schemes)
7 Mansfield St. London W1M OAT tel: 0207 636 6541

For advice on epilepsy in Collies, contact:

The Canine Epilepsy Support Group
22 St. Eric's Rd., Bessacarr, Doncaster DN4 6NG tel 01302 536090 / 719322

Anyone interested in complementary remedies for a range of canine health conditions should contact Barbara Swann (details listed under Midlands Border Collie Club).

Also see **Old Wives' and Dogs'** Tales by Linda Adam (£5.99 Broadcast Books) for her collection of tried and tested traditional, natural remedies for minor pet ailments.

Collie Shows and Competitions

To find out more on local training clubs, Agility clubs, Working Trials Societies, Ringcraft Clubs, etc., contact **The Kennel Club** (details under Breeders Section). For advice on how to put your Collie on The Kennel Club's Working Trial and Obedience Register, call them on 0207 493 2001. Shows are regularly advertised in the following weekly canine publications:

Dog World
Somerfield House
Wotton Rd
Ashford, Kent TN23 6LW

Our Dogs
5 Oxford Rd,
Station Approach
Manchester M1 8DP

In addition, magazines such as **Agility Voice** or **Agility Eye** cover Agility events. **Working Trials Monthly** caters for trials devotees, and **Dog Training Weekly** carries details of Obedience events and news.

Index